ADVANCED LINKEDIN

For your Job Search, Business, and Career

By Robert Hellmann, President of *Hellmann Career Consulting*,
www.hellmannconsulting.com

Published by:
Robert Hellmann LLC, New York, USA

THANK YOU FOR YOUR PURCHASE

TABLE OF CONTENTS

ABOUT THE AUTHOR

As President of **Hellmann Career Consulting**, Robert Hellmann provides a range of services to individuals and organizations, including career coaching, executive coaching, workshops and organizational consulting.

He holds certifications with the Five O'Clock Club as a Senior Career and Executive Coach, and with LinkedIn as a Certified Professional Recruiter. In addition to his private coaching practice, Rob has served as an adjunct instructor at New York University teaching career management, and as the Five O'Clock Club's Vice President and Associate Director of its Guild of Career Coaches. He has developed key aspects of the Club's coach certification curriculum, and regularly coaches their most senior c-level clients.

Rob is a sought-after speaker, and has given hundreds of seminars on career, recruiting and employee engagement topics to corporations, higher-education institutions, professional associations, and government/non-profit organizations. Rob also regularly leads top-rated employee workshops on "Presentation Skills," "LinkedIn for Business" and "Recruiting for Results."

Rob is a regular contributor to *Forbes*. His insights have also appeared in media outlets such as *The New York Times, The Wall Street Journal, the Washington Post, the Chicago Tribune, CBS News, CNNMoney, ABC News, NBC News, WPIX News, Consumer Reports, Glassdoor.com* and many others.

Rob authored the books *Peak Presentations* and *The Social Media Boost,* and has contributed three chapters to the Five O'Clock Club's book *Work Smarts* on leadership, performance management, and mentoring.

Rob's background includes over 20 years of experience in Career Development, Organizational Development, Finance and Marketing, with clients and employers including American Express, JP Morgan Chase, the Federal Reserve Bank of New York, and the Audubon Society. He has developed career services programs for organizations including Columbia University, Harvard Business School, New York University, Fordham University, Montclair State University and more.

Active in non-profits, Rob has co-led the Career Development arm of the Marketing Executives Networking Group (MENG) and served on the board of the Association for Talent Development's New York City chapter; he currently co-leads their Career Development SIG. Rob's educational background includes a BS in Economics/Math from Binghamton University and an MBA in Finance from Fordham University.

As a career and executive coach, Rob has helped thousands of clients to define and achieve their career goals, develop as managers and leaders, and navigate through challenging work situations. In his private coaching practice, Rob combines a warm, empowering style with a pragmatic, bottom-line focus that gets results for clients in the shortest possible time. Feel free to contact him at rob@hellmannconsulting.com, or visit his website at www.hellmannconsulting.com.

"One must never consent to creep when one has the impulse to soar"
Helen Keller

This book is dedicated to
all those who seek to be the architects of their own destiny.

HOW THIS BOOK IS ORGANIZED

This book starts with the basics. If you've never tried or hardly use LinkedIn, you will find out how to unlock its value. For those more experienced with LinkedIn, we go way beyond the basics, covering advanced features that will advance your career, whether you're in a job search, seeking success in your current job, or looking to build a business.

Much of getting set up on and using LinkedIn is the same regardless of how you plan to use it. Chapters one, two and three are targeted to all readers; minor variations in strategy or approach relevant to jobseekers, business-builders or on-the-job advancers are called out as appropriate.

Some features and strategies, however, are uniquely suited to only one of these three reader groups. Chapter four focuses on the needs of jobseekers. Chapter five covers the unique needs of those seeking to build a business or succeed in their current positions.

Finally, I seek to place LinkedIn in a larger context. In the last third of this book, we discuss how LinkedIn compares to Twitter, Facebook, and other social media platforms. I also include a thorough explanation of how to use Twitter in conjunction with "Social Media Managers."

LinkedIn is great for finding the "right" people to contact. But what do you say once you've found them? Well, in the Appendix I've included sections on how to write great emails and cover letters, so that you boost the odds of getting the response you are hoping for.

This book is also available in digital form as an eBook. Once you have purchased this paperback version, you can **download the latest version of the eBook for free** (it's updated as needed throughout the year). Just follow the instructions in the Appendix, on page 141 of this book.

If you have any comments or suggestions for future editions, or you want to share your results from using this guide, I would appreciate hearing from you at rob@hellmannconsulting.com.

Thanks for your interest, and best wishes on reaching your career goals!

INTRODUCTION

"If content is king, then conversation is queen."
John Munsell

Gone are the days when simply responding to ads was enough to get a good job quickly, or just doing your job well was enough to keep it. And as a growing number try their hand at business (the "self-employed" economy), business competition becomes that much fiercer. Today, you need to know how to use every tool in your arsenal to reach your career goals.

LinkedIn is a thoroughly proven job search and career management aid. If your job targets, clients or customers are well represented on LinkedIn, you should be active on this platform. Those who really know how to use LinkedIn find that they reach their career and business goals faster.

Yet career-advancers who haven't used LinkedIn effectively span generations. Often younger clients feel that Facebook or Instagram alone is enough (it's not), or LinkedIn is for "older people" as one college senior remarked (I told him he's about to join that club!). More seasoned clients are put off by the learning curve. Even those comfortable using these applications are often unaware of powerful career advancement features.

I share this book with career-advancers of all ages so they know how to boost their effectiveness using LinkedIn to land jobs, clients, careers, promotions, or to build their business, putting them ahead of their less LinkedIn-savvy competitors.

Why should you read this book?
This guide stems from my work as a career and executive coach with an active practice. I bring insights based on daily experience with powerful techniques that will help you to reach your career goals. My recommendations incorporate learning from my own research, from client experiences, and from my partnership with LinkedIn on leading workshops for their *LinkedIn Recruiter* platform. They also incorporate a highly effective, field-tested approach to the job search: the *Five*

O'Clock Club career advancement methodology (see Appendix for more information). I'm certified in this methodology, co-lead its refinement, and have leveraged it in helping thousands of clients land jobs and advance in their careers.

This book also highlights when you should incorporate specific social media applications. For some it can be tempting to jump right on the social media bandwagon with wild abandon. But since you are on a mission to get the job, clients or career you want, you need to take a more thoughtful approach. This book shows you how to prioritize the use of LinkedIn within your larger career- or business-building effort, so you don't waste time, and use your precious time productively.

Lastly, I've shared many client examples and case studies. Much of this book involves step-by-step "how-to" instructions. Reviewing the experiences of clients who've followed these steps should make this approach resonate.

Early form of Social Media

1. WHAT IS LINKEDIN, AND WHY SHOULD YOU CARE?

*"**Six degrees of separation** refers to the idea that everyone is at most six steps away from any other person on Earth…"*
(**Wikipedia**)

LinkedIn, accessed at www.linkedin.com, enables users to keep in touch with and expand their professional networks, get introductions to others outside their immediate network, and join groups of professionals organized around industries, professions, and associations.

The "culture" of LinkedIn is all about advancing your professional career or business. With a global membership in the hundreds of millions, the site is well designed to make it easy to develop and maintain professional relationships. Hiring managers, in-house recruiters, recruiting firms and potential customers are using LinkedIn to scan profiles for viable candidates.

The free version of LinkedIn has been useful to jobseekers, business-builders and career advancers at all levels. One client in business development successfully used LinkedIn to simultaneously obtain sales-prospect meetings and land interviews for a career change! He ultimately made his sought-after career transition through a contact he made in a LinkedIn group (more about groups in Chapter 2, "Getting Set Up"). These positive results are typical for clients who know how to use LinkedIn.

Why Use LinkedIn?

Throughout your search, you want to have a presence in places where you can connect with people who can help you. LinkedIn is such a place. Use it to connect to people who can hire you, refer you, buy from you, or provide information about your prospects. LinkedIn tends to attract those whose professions are characterized by periodic job changes (including consultants) or entrepreneurs looking for an audience.

You also want to be in a place where people and organizations are looking for someone with your abilities. LinkedIn is such a place. Almost all recruiters use LinkedIn to source candidates. For many hiring managers, LinkedIn is a first stop to fill an open position; they check first to see who in their network might be suitable before going to HR or a search firm for help.

If you sell products or services, LinkedIn can help you to be found as well if your target market is represented on LinkedIn (many prospective clients have found me by searching on LinkedIn). Since Google indexes LinkedIn profiles in their search results, an active LinkedIn presence will also help you to be found via Google searches.

Although many professions are represented well on LinkedIn, those with very low job turnover have a smaller presence. Primary or secondary school teachers are an example. Conversations with colleagues in your target market (or quick searches on LinkedIn itself) can help you to decide whether to prioritize LinkedIn for your career. In most cases, the answer will be "yes."

The free version of LinkedIn, on which most of this book focuses, enables you to do the following easily and effectively:

- **Develop and maintain a network** of people who can help your career or business.
- **Get introductions** to people in organizations where you would like to work via your network.
- **Contact "strangers"** directly for information or meetings.
- **Research people, companies, industries and professions** to prepare for meetings or learn more about a job target or prospect.
- **Identify key hiring managers, prospects or influencers** at an organization so that you can contact them. Finding these people, often a difficult part of the search, is made easier on LinkedIn.
- **Respond to job postings** more effectively; bypass the glut of applications for a typical job posting.

- **Maintain a presence** in a location where **recruiters** or others in need of your services search for help. Your LinkedIn presence is also boosts your visibility in Google search results.
- **Build a following** for your business products or services.

LinkedIn Terms

1st Degree Network: the people you connect with directly.
2nd Degree Network: the people who connect directly with your 1st degree network.
3rd Degree Network: the people who connect directly with your 2nd degree network.
Group: LinkedIn members who congregate in an organized LinkedIn forum around a specific topic, profession, or association.

Your 1st degree network includes people who have accepted your invitation to connect, or sent you an invitation that you have accepted. Your 1st degree network can introduce you to people in your 2nd degree network, and indirectly to people in your 3rd degree network. See the chart below for what my network looked like a few years back. I had connected to 381 people directly, which theoretically enabled me to get introductions to almost 5.2 million people!

Your Network of Trusted Professionals

You are at the center of your network. Your connections can introduce you to 5,190,400+ professionals — here's how your network breaks down:

1 **Your Connections** Your trusted friends and colleagues		381
2 **Two degrees away** Friends of friends; each connected to one of your connections		116,600+
3 **Three degrees away** Reach these users through a friend and one of their friends		5,073,400+
Total users you can contact through an Introduction		5,190,400+

But I effectively have access to far more than 5.2 million people, because of the power of LinkedIn Groups; in most cases, you can message anyone within a group that you share. Note: You can also message anyone in your LinkedIn 1st degree network, but you cannot directly message your 2nd or 3rd degree network. You need to be introduced to a 2nd degree connection through your 1st degree, or send a paid LinkedIn message, called an "InMail," to your 2nd or 3rd degree connection.

The sections that follow explain how to
1. Get set up on LinkedIn, and then
2. Use LinkedIn's powerful features for finding and contacting people, keeping in touch, and even building a following.

OK, now put on your LinkedIn swimsuit, and let's dive in!

**The Next Step in
Social Media's Evolution**

2. GETTING SET-UP ON LINKEDIN

In this Chapter:

✓ To get the most out of LinkedIn, you will need the following:
  - o A powerful LinkedIn Profile
  - o A "great" network
  - o Membership in a number relevant of groups
✓ If you have your own business, you may also want to set up a Company Page.
✓ LinkedIn's "Settings" are important for visibility and privacy.

Go to www.LinkedIn.com for your free log-on ID and password. Once you log in, follow the prompts to begin creating your profile and inviting people to connect with you.

Early on you will be prompted with options to send your contacts LinkedIn invitations and build your network quickly by importing all your contacts from your online or desktop address book. **I would advise skipping these steps for now.** You want to build a decent LinkedIn profile first before inviting people to connect with you. When finished with these initial prompts, you will notice that you are on the Home page, as indicated by the highlighted word on the top menu. Click on the "Me" menu option at the top of the page, then "View Profile," as shown in the picture that follows (you'll find these icons at the top of every page. You're now ready to create your profile.

NOTE: LinkedIn made major changes to its user interface in early 2017. This book reflects these changes. Going forward, you can expect LinkedIn to periodically modify its menu structure while keeping 99% of the functionality; the result will usually be an extra minute or two to find out where a particular menu option now resides, with the worst case being a trip to "Help" (found by clicking on the "Me" icon, your tiny picture at the top right of a page).

LinkedIn Settings

Before you are going to write (or re-write) your profile, set your visibility settings so no one in your network will get notified of changes to your profile in their Home page "feed" or periodic network activity emails. You don't want people to check out your profile when it's not ready! There's only one chance to make a good first impression. And, if you are connected to your boss and in a job search, you may not want to spark her curiosity with a notification of changes to your profile.

To temporarily prevent your network from being notified of changes, once again click on the tiny "Me" picture on the upper right, then select "Settings and Privacy," then click "Privacy," and finally click on "Sharing profile edits" as pictured below.

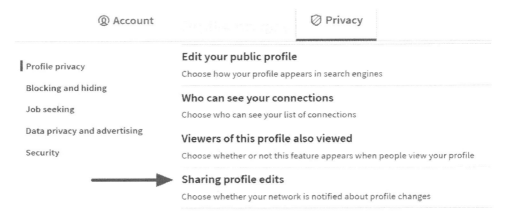

Switch this option to No.

Once your profile is in reasonably good shape, reset this switch to "Yes" for maximum visibility; if you are in (or contemplating) a job search or are building a business, notifications of your now occasional profile updates can help to remind your network of your services.

Other Settings

On this same page and the two adjoining "Account" and "Communications" tabs, I would recommend you review the other settings and know what the options are, as you may want to change your settings regarding privacy, how and when you are contacted, your visibility on LinkedIn, and how you notify others of profile changes.

In this same Privacy section, another setting you would want to change right away is: *Edit your public profile*. This section allows you to, among other things, select an easy-to-remember URL, by entering one under "Customize this Address." This friendlier URL can now be used in your resume or in your email signature. For example, originally, the link to my profile was something like: http://www.linkedin.com/pub/Robert-Hellmann/21a8244. I was able to change it to www.linkedin.com/in/roberthellmann.

Make your completed public profile as visible as you can. I recommend the default "Full View" once you feel your profile is in good shape—that is, check-off all the boxes associated with the visibility of various parts of your profile. If you feel uncomfortable with this, you can alter details of what is visible in this section.

Privacy – Blocking a User

When you block a user, you become invisible to them on LinkedIn, and they become invisible to you. Up to 50 LinkedIn users can be blocked. In that same Privacy tab, scroll down to "Blocking and Hiding" and then select "Blocking."

The rest of the settings are straightforward so you don't need me to walk you through it. I will, however, cover certain settings later on.

Creating a Powerful LinkedIn Profile

Most LinkedIn users will want to construct a profile using basic resume-writing principles, regardless of whether or not they're in a job search (there is one exception for some business owners-- see Chapter 5, *For Your Business*). If you have a well-crafted resume already, I recommend cutting and pasting your resume directly into the corresponding LinkedIn sections, assuming the exceptions that I'm about to describe don't require you to significantly alter it. In particular,

✓ Write your profile (as you do your resume) for the specific audience that you want to reach, that is, the people who could hire you in your job target or give you business.

✓ Use phrasing and keywords that will resonate with your target audience.

✓ Use clear, concise, to-the-point language. Although LinkedIn doesn't easily give you a bullet-point option, you can use dashes or asterisks as a substitute, to help create a tight feel. You can also copy/paste bullet points and symbols from Microsoft Word into your profile.

✓ Make your profile accomplishment-oriented when appropriate; include the impact of what you did, not just your responsibilities. For example, say "increased sales by 23%" or "substantially improved efficiency." I tell clients to always seek to write accomplishment-oriented bullets.

✓ Your profile should not be a laundry list of everything you've done. Instead only include the experience that applies to your target audience, and exclude or minimize experience that doesn't.

✓ Have a strong Summary Section, essentially your greatest hits or "pitch," at the top of your profile. Click the "Add new profile section" button on the top right of your profile page and then select "Summary."

Add new profile section

When your profile needs to differ from your resume

Keep these four differences in mind as you adapt your resume to your profile; They may require you to make significant changes to your resume content, to make it work for your profile.

Only one profile, so you need to choose
Spreading your network across multiple profiles is impractical and confusing (unlike your resume, where you can and should have a different resume for each job target). Having only one profile means that you will have to decide whether to go more general, to encompass multiple target audiences, or to focus your profile on your primary target only.

Your decision will depend on your specific situation. I recommend writing your profile for your primary target, IF it won't "cost" you too much. By focusing on one target, you avoid the risk that your profile will be too broad, not appealing to any one audience.

By cost, however, I mean missed opportunities or puzzled looks from your boss or colleagues who wonder why your profile says something very different from what you are currently doing! For example, I had a client who was a financial controller, but had substantial information technology experience as well. He wanted to move into an IT role, so we wrote his resume to focus on his IT experience and leadership, and de-emphasize his financial controller background. He was also looking to build an IT consulting business on the side.

But, because he was connected to his boss and a number of other work colleagues on LinkedIn, he could not write the profile the same way as his resume. His boss might have become suspicious when viewing his IT-focused profile, since my client was a financial controller! So, we had to broaden the profile language beyond the language used in his resume, to encompass both his finance and IT experience.

Warning: In case you accidentally open up more than one profile/account (search under your name if you are unsure), close one down to avoid major confusion in building and updating your network (Note: You cannot transfer connections from one account to another). Consult LinkedIn "Help" to learn the steps involved in closing an account.

Your Profile has a broader viewing audience
Listing certain specific accomplishments that are on your resume may not be a good idea because of the profile's broader viewing audience. You will need to be the judge of when it is or isn't appropriate. One way around this that might work for you is to use percentages instead of raw numbers on your profile. For example, one client had "Increased revenue by $10 million to $48 million" on her resume. For her LinkedIn profile, she changed this to "Increased revenue by 26%."

Having a Profile doesn't mean you are looking for opportunities
While your resume equals "job search," the same is not true for your LinkedIn profile. So, if you are in fact looking for a job or consulting engagement, should you indicate that you are actively doing so on your profile? The short answer is no.

Now for the long answer. I have known situations where people have been contacted for opportunities with statements in their profile that artfully indicate their search, e.g. "Seeking next exciting challenge" or "Open to select new opportunities." On the other hand, I have talked to recruiters and hiring managers who say that there still is a bias against people who are perceived as out of work and actively searching. In fact, recent research has backed this claim up—see this article in *the Atlantic*: http://bit.ly/192Zqs6 . So a statement indicating you are looking for a job can be divisive; some may be encouraged to contact you, while others will be discouraged.

For these reasons, statements that make it clear you are looking for a job should be left out of a profile. And especially, don't make these two (way too common) profile mistakes:

DON'T: Indicate your openness to opportunities in your 120-character Headline. On LinkedIn, this limited space is valuable real-estate, since it is what people see when they view people-search results. In addition, LinkedIn places a heavy weight on keywords placed in this area when prioritizing profiles to display in search results. Therefore, use this very limited space to pitch an employer with your expertise and brand differentiation-- don't waste it!

DON'T: Put the words "unemployed" or "looking for a job" on your profile. These "negative" phrases will turn off a potential employer.

Some clients ask me, "If I don't say I'm searching for opportunities in my profile, how will a recruiter, hiring manager, or consulting prospect know that I'm available?" I tell them not to worry about it. Anyone who uses LinkedIn to source candidates (both hiring managers and recruiters) knows to contact people who fit the bill but may not be currently looking. In fact, I know from training recruiters that there is often a bias in favor of these "passive" candidates!

In addition, for jobseekers, whether to include these statements goes to the heart of how you approach your search. I advocate an active approach to the job search, one where you are going out and getting what you want, not waiting to be found. If you take this approach, indicating that you are looking for a job on your profile becomes less important.

That said, there are better ways to indicate you are open to opportunities without stating it outright and risking turning people off. For example:

- The word "consulting" in your current job title or description indicates, by its very nature, that you are open to other opportunities. Some of you may be in a situation where you can use this word.

- You "may" be able to include in your current position the services you offer employers. For example, you could say something like: "Services include:…" and then list your services in bullet points. Be careful with this if you are not in business for yourself and are employed full time!

The tone of your profile can differ from your resume

Because LinkedIn is part of the "social" media universe, it is OK for the profile language to be a bit more informal than your resume's language. What this means in practice is that you can choose to start off bullets with either:

- Action verbs such as "Created… Led…" where the personal pronouns "I" and "my" are left out.
  OR
- Personal pronouns like "I Created" and "My experience." This more informal format is not appropriate for resumes, but works well for social media liked LinkedIn. That said, keep your tone professional and appropriate for your target.

On some profiles I see people using "third person" language, i.e. "Armando Rafiy is an accomplished project manager…" That language feels too formal given the social-media nature of LinkedIn and you may be perceived as too old fashioned.

In addition to these differences, LinkedIn profiles contain sections to add additional information that don't have a corresponding place in your resume. Some of these are described in the sections that follow.

Editing Your Profile

When you first go into LinkedIn, you are on your "Home" page, where you can see your network's activity and post your own activity. To view and edit your profile, click on the "Me" icon by the tiny picture of you on the top right (if you don't have a picture yet, it will show up as a grey blank circle).

Here's where I would click on my Home page to view and edit my profile. Another way: click on the big picture of you near the top left of your Home page to get to your profile.

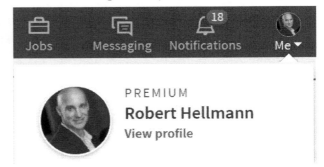

Editing Profile Sections

You can edit any section by clicking on the pencil icon.   In most sections, you can add or link to media, such as a video or a file. While currently you can't change the position of profile sections, you can change the order of specific work experiences (more on that shortly).

How to Be Found

Your profile's content and completeness is key to your being ranked highly in the search results of potential employers, clients, customers or collaborators.

Be "Relevant"

When people enter keywords to search for potential employees, consultants, presenters, etc. LinkedIn's search results default to a sort "By Relevance." LinkedIn defines relevance by a combination of keyword presence, strength of connections and strength of profile completeness. Specifically, here's how LinkedIn orders searches by keyword sorted by Relevance:

1. LinkedIn first sorts by degree of connection. "1st degree connections" are the category of people that show up at the top of a search, then 2nd, then groups, then 3rd degree, and finally everyone else.

---

2. Within each of the sort categories in #1 above, people are then sorted by the degree of profile completeness, with the most complete profiles at the top of each category.

This sort order tells us that 1) having a larger network will increase the likelihood of showing up in searches, and 2) having a complete profile is very important as well to showing up in searches. While LinkedIn's sorting approach might suggest to you that you should connect with everyone and anyone, this is not necessarily the case. While quantity of connections is clearly important, the quality of connections should, for most of us, be prioritized before quantity. See the "Strategy for Connecting" section that follows on page 34 to learn why.

Have a Complete Profile

Just below the top-most "Intro" section, on the left side, you will see a profile strength indicator. If it says anything less than "All Star" you need to make your profile more complete so that you come up higher in search results. Also, your profile will in general be more impactful if you follow LinkedIn's suggestions for profile completeness. You can access these suggestions by clicking on "Add New Profile Sections" just to the right of the Intro section. See the following picture.

From LinkedIn's blog, LinkedIn considers these items to contribute to maximum profile strength:

- Adding a photo
- Listing "all of your" jobs or positions that you've held (*I take this to mean one or more jobs*)

- Including a description in the jobs or positions that you have listed
- Having five or more skills on your profile
- Filling out the Summary section
- Including your industry
- Adding where you went to school
- Having 50 or more connections

Guide to Profile Sections

Below are guidelines for filling out select profile sections. You can add items within a section, or edit sections, by clicking the "+" icon or pencil icon, respectively.

The Intro Section: This is the top-most section on your LinkedIn profile, and it's the first thing people see when they look at your profile. So make it good! This section has some key components.

Headline: This is the line that appears just under your picture. Fill in this part using the 120 characters allowed. Describe how people should categorize you, and if room is left, what makes you different from the competition.

For example, if you are targeting Project Management roles in financial technology, you might say:

Project Manager, FinTech | PMP Certified • IT/Business Unit Liaison • Product Launches • Six Sigma Black Belt

Project Manager, Financial Technology is the category, and the rest is the differentiation. **Use Keywords** (see the next section, "Add Keywords" for more information).

Here's another keyword-rich example for a Human Resources Business Partner. I asked my client "What would people type into LinkedIn to search for someone with your skills?" That's how we came up with many of the keywords in this headline.

Human Resources Business Partner | Strategy • Performance Mgmt • Talent Acquisition & Development • Total Rewards • Employee Engagement

Photo: Definitely add a photo, and make it appropriate for your target audience. A photo adds warmth, doesn't look like your hiding something, and counts towards profile completeness which helps with search rankings. When a potential employer or client finds you and doesn't see a photo, they are less likely to click on you given that most other profiles they find will have a photo (LinkedIn's research supports this). If you want you can add a photo stored on your smartphone by installing the LinkedIn app and clicking on the photo icon from the app.

Summary: This section is an expanded version of your Headline. Include your "greatest hits" from among your accomplishments, preferably in bullet form. See my profile as an example: www.linkedin.com/in/roberthellmann. Note that when looking at someone's profile, only the first two lines of the summary section are initially visible. You need to click the dropdown arrow to view the whole summary. The first two lines of your summary, then, take on exaggerated importance, so craft them with care.

If you represent your company to external audiences, e.g. as a recruiter or sales-person, you should also add one or two sentences in your Summary that express why your employer or its product/service is so great. Adding this language will both help you succeed in your current role and suggest to potential future employers that you would "sell" them effectively as well. For example, one client added a couple of sentences that began with: "As a customer success manager, I'm excited to be a part of a forward-thinking technology company such as TechCo, where I have the opportunity to provide cutting edge solutions to client challenges."

The Experience Section: Start with your current or most recent position. Add your education as well. LinkedIn will use the organization names you enter to suggest people you may know—helpful in building your network.

If you are unemployed, consider listing yourself as a consultant (e.g. "Jane Doe Consulting") if you have done anything work-related at all since your last job—even if you were not paid for it. Volunteering is work experience (often requiring more skills than your paying gig); you don't need to advertise that you "volunteered," i.e. were paid zero to do this work!

If you are looking for a job, try to put something in that current job slot if possible. From my experience teaching LinkedIn to recruiters I know many of them use the "current job title" field in their searches, so if you have no current title you won't show up.

If you worked at one organization for a long time and held several positions, you will have to decide whether each of those positions should occupy a separate organization "slot" in your profile, or all your positions should fall under one organization heading. There is no one right answer. Here are the factors to consider:
- Will all the position descriptions/accomplishments fit within the 2,000-character limit for one organization slot?
- How different are the positions?
- Having your long organizational tenure split among several slots:
   o Makes it harder for the reader to quickly discern your longevity at one company, and long tenure is usually a positive.
   o Enables you to add more keyword-rich job titles.

Re-order your experiences: LinkedIn allows you to re-order your positions so they don't have to follow a strictly chronological order. This ability can be very useful, especially if you're a consultant and have more than one "job" or you want to highlight the amazing job you had just before your current one.

Recommendations: Skip this for now—they are important, but you are not ready to receive (or give) them yet, since only people you are connected to can give you recommendations.

Featured Skills and Endorsements: Use this section to enter up to 50 keywords, the more the better, as your chances of being "found" will increase. You can also re-order your skills to ensure the most relevant ones are on-top. Don't worry about endorsements for now, we'll discuss these later in the book.

Contact and Personal Info: You can edit these settings in the upper right column.

For Students with Little Work History: Add sections tailored to you, e.g. Projects, Honors & Awards, Courses, Organizations, and Test Scores.

Add Keywords

Keywords, that is, words that people may use to conduct LinkedIn searches, help your search ranking more in some parts of your profile than others. In particular, keywords in your **Name** (i.e. if they are searching for your name), **Headline, Company Name, Job Title** and **Skills** are weighted heavily in search results.

For Company Name, make sure you chose the organization name LinkedIn recognizes; you'll see the company logo appear if that's the case (assuming your company has a LinkedIn Company Page, as most do- see page 88 for more on Company Pages). If LinkedIn recognizes the company, it will suggest you to others who worked there, and it will suggest them to you, helping you to be found and build your network.

Nevertheless, keywords do matter everywhere in your profile, which is one reason why it is so important to have a 100% complete profile. If these key fields are blank or filled with generic terms, then you fall to the bottom of the search rankings.

LinkedIn's various features can help you to identify keywords for both your profile and your resume. I recommend three approaches for researching keywords:

Do an "Advanced Job-postings Search"
Make use of LinkedIn's broad and deep listing of job-postings to identify relevant keywords, whether you are in a job search, looking for consulting gigs, or researching business prospects. Click on "Jobs" in the top menu, type some initial search information, then click search. You'll then see results along with a column on the right that allows you to further refine your results. Enter parameters that represent job postings in which you may be interested.

For example, if you are looking for a Marketing Director position in the Marketing and Advertising sector, you can enter in the Title field:

"Marketing AND Director NOT (analysis OR analytics)"

Note, the connectors (AND, OR, NOT) must be capitalized. Then, select the appropriate industry.

The result: you will find job postings for the industry you selected that have these keywords in the posting title. Then you can refine your search further using additional search filters that appear in the right column, including industry, job function, experience level, company name, and more.

Once you have found two or three postings that match your job target, review them to look for keywords. For example, when I performed this exact search, I found additional keywords like "digital marketing," "cross-channel marketing," "communications," and "campaigns."

Create a "Word Cloud" for the Job Postings you found
Word clouds enable you to visually see the frequency of words that show up in a block of text. If you google "Word Cloud" you will see the many free tools that can enable you to create word clouds.

I use "TagCrowd" at www.tagcrowd.com; With this application, just copy the job description text from each of the two or three postings that you found into the TagCrowd input box, checking off "100 words maximum" and "show frequency." Then click "visualize" and relevant keywords jump out in the resulting word-cloud.

Do an "Advanced People Search"
Click inside the search box at the top of any page, then click on the magnifying glass that appears.

You will now be in "Advanced Search." Click "people" from the resulting menu options to conduct an Advanced People Search.

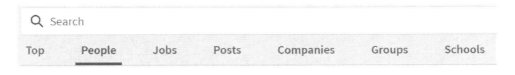

On the right you will see the "Filter by" options. Scroll down for the "Keywords" dropdown and click on it.

You will see options to filter by job title. Enter the same search criteria that you used for Title in the "Advanced Job-postings Search." Browse through the LinkedIn profiles of those people that you found through this search, with a specific focus on the "skills" section of their profile, to identify keywords.

By the way, I discuss the <u>Advanced People Search</u> feature in more detail in Chapter 3, *Using LinkedIn.*

Check out Relevant Company Pages
For business owners, consultants and jobseekers, company pages can be another valuable source of keywords. Look up the companies that represent your job targets, potential clients or competitors, and incorporate the keywords you find as appropriate. It's easy to do this: just select "Companies" from the advanced search options menu and start typing a company name into the search window.

Q Search						
Top	People	Jobs	Posts	**Companies**	Groups	Schools

Test Your Profile's "Searchability"

Incorporate the most relevant keywords that you have come up with throughout your profile, including the Headline, Job Titles and Skills section. Ensure you're not "keyword stuffing" in an obvious way; you need to display a polished, professional image. Now search LinkedIn using those keywords. For example, if you think people will look for you by entering "Graphic Designer" then type these words in quotes (so LinkedIn sees it as a phrase) in the People Search box, as shown in the following picture.

Q "graphic designer"						
Top	People	Jobs	Posts	Companies	Groups	Schools

If you don't show up on the first page of results, look at the profiles of those that do to find additional keywords. Update your profile to include more relevant terms and then search again.

For example, if your current job title says "Consultant," change it to "Graphic Design Consultant." You'll actually see yourself moving up the ranks each time you improve the number and placement of your keywords. If you are a business owner and your job title says "President," that's not helping your search rankings! Replace "President" with a functional job description, e.g. "Marketing Consultant: Social Media, Digital Marketing, eCommerce."

Get and Give Recommendations

Go to https://www.linkedin.com/recs/ to manage the recommendations you get and give, including deciding which ones to accept and hide, as well as determine the display order.

You can get recommendations from people in your 1st degree network by sending out a recommendation request from this section, or by going to their profile and clicking the three dots on the top right of their "Intro" section.

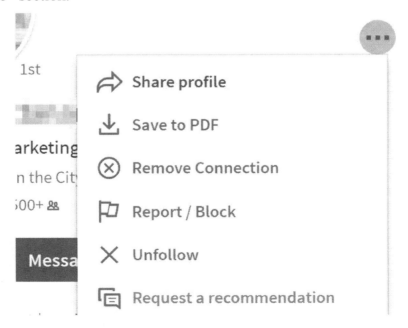

These recommendations enhance your marketability.

When you request the recommendation, include in your request the areas of your experience that you want emphasized. This will make it easier for the person to write the recommendation, and you are more likely to get a high-quality one. Once a person writes a recommendation, you will be notified by email. You can then choose whether to accept it, ask for a revision, ignore or decline it.

Do not accept weak recommendations, as they can potentially hurt you. For example, one of my clients received a recommendation that read: "I worked with Marion for two years. Marion did budgeting for our division. She is very detail oriented." The content is factual, but does not indicate how well Marion did her job, leaving this question hanging uncomfortably. Much stronger would be: "Marion did a great job ensuring that the budget was completed accurately, and on schedule."

People may also ask you for a recommendation. If you feel positive about the person, I would encourage you to write it. Beyond it being a generous thing to do, the number of recommendations you both gave and received also shows up on your profile; giving recommendations looks impressive!

Lastly, you can select the order with which your recommendations appear, by going to 'Manage Recommendations' in LinkedIn Settings. Choose the order based on some combination of recommendation recency and quality.

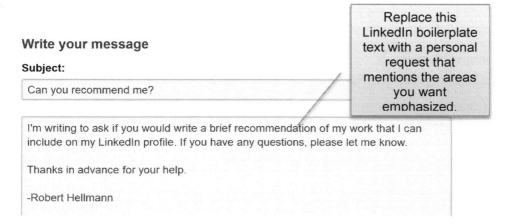

Replace this LinkedIn boilerplate text with a personal request that mentions the areas you want emphasized.

Write your message

Subject:

Can you recommend me?

I'm writing to ask if you would write a brief recommendation of my work that I can include on my LinkedIn profile. If you have any questions, please let me know.

Thanks in advance for your help.

-Robert Hellmann

Endorsements vs. Recommendations

LinkedIn has an "Endorsements" feature that many (including myself) find problematic because the "endorse" button is too easy to click on. The result is too many endorsements for things that you actually did not help the endorsers with, which reduces the feature's value. Recruiters and they consistently disparage this feature, discounting it in their decision-making process, for this reason. On the other hand, LinkedIn Recommendations are valued by recruiters both because of the effort involved and the more descriptive nature of the recommendations.

So, should you bother to get endorsements? Don't go out of your way, for the reasons I describe above. BUT, if you have a lot of endorsements, it does look like you have at least something going for you, i.e. you are good at getting endorsements! Plus, it suggests that those who endorsed you like (or don't dislike) you. In that sense, lots of endorsements can add something positive to your profile.

Personally, I wish LinkedIn never added the Endorsements feature. Recommendations are more than enough. But if you're motivated, then a lot of endorsements will only help you. That said, my "recommendation" is to prioritize your valuable time by prioritizing getting recommendations over endorsements, since recommendations are way more impressive. All other things equal, my feeling is that 10 strong recommendations are worth 500 endorsements.

Here's what the Skills and Endorsements section looks like.

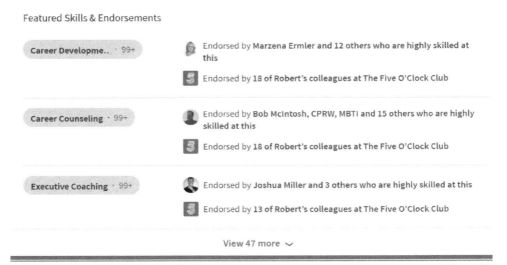

LinkedIn's "Who's Viewed Your Profile" Feature

LinkedIn gives users the ability to see who is checking out their profile; "Free" LinkedIn provides a snapshot of the most recent profile viewers, while "Paid" LinkedIn gives far more history on profile views. You can access this feature on the left column of your home page.

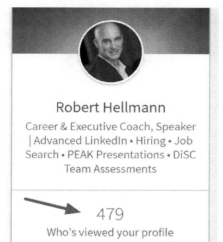

Robert Hellmann

Career & Executive Coach, Speaker | Advanced LinkedIn • Hiring • Job Search • PEAK Presentations • DiSC Team Assessments

479

Who's viewed your profile

Many jobseekers and business owners get fixated on this feature. They are hoping that an employer or potential client is looking for them, and are thinking "this person checked me out, what could it mean? Should I reach out to them?"

The approach I recommend is to make reaching out to someone who viewed your profile only a small part of your career management approach. By definition, waiting to see who's viewed your profile is a passive, reactive approach. I have seen over and over again that the most successful jobseekers and business owners are the ones who actively seek out opportunities. They don't wait around for people to find them, but proactively reach out to potential employers and clients to land meetings and interviews.

That said, if used judiciously, this feature could be helpful. If you see the "right" person from an organization on your marketing plan checking out your profile without you having reached out, it might be worth an email. See the section in Chapter 3, page 58, How to Contact People for more information on how to reach out. Keep in mind, though, that they haven't contacted you despite looking at your profile, so weigh carefully whether it's really worth spending your precious career management time on someone who likely may not be interested! From experience, in most cases it's not worth the effort.

Building Your LinkedIn Network

Now that you have a decent profile, you can start to build your network and your visibility. One of LinkedIn's primary values is in its ability to both keep you "connected" with your **1st degree network**, and get you introduced to your **2nd and 3rd degree extended network**.

Strategy for Connecting

For most professions, job searches, and businesses, the best strategy for developing your LinkedIn network is **quality first, then quantity** (with some exceptions discussed in the next section). Quality means:

a) You know them in some way (even if only barely) and you might be open to helping them/they might be open to helping you. This category includes, for example, a) someone with whom you had a good 20-minute conversation at a conference and want to keep in touch, b) someone you worked with 10 years ago, haven't talked to since, and you were at least on cordial terms way back when, c) family, friends, your dentist, etc.

b) You don't know them, but they reach out to you first and after looking at their profile, you want them in your network. You will want to selectively accept requests to connect from people you don't know, if their background, connections or character make them someone who you would welcome in your network. The reason: because they initiated the request to connect, they are self-selecting for being more open to facilitating an introduction on your behalf.

Since I like to know everyone in my network, i.e. have a quality network based on real relationships, here's what I do when I get a request from someone I don't know, and I'm open to connecting with them. I first accept their connection request. Then I send them a LinkedIn message (just click "message" right from their profile) that goes something like this: Subject: Nice to be connected to you! Body: *"I appreciate your invite to connect! As I like to know everyone in my first-degree network, I'm curious as to what prompted you to reach out to me and/or how you come across my profile."*

If they never bother to respond to this message, then I will "remove" them as a connection (by just clicking on the three dots to the right of their picture and selecting "Remove

Connection"). On the other hand, most people will respond, and I've built some great new professional relationships this way!

One client already had thousands of connections when we began working together. When he tried using LinkedIn to find people to whom he could reach out, he found the experience frustrating because the quality of his network was poor. He had just been randomly accepting connection requests to build quantity. Yet reaching out to these strangers for introductions was not productive—most could care less about him! In addition, the network updates LinkedIn sent to his inbox and his Home page feed were meaningless to him. Ultimately, he removed many connections and LinkedIn began to be more useful.

Once you have established "quality," then "quantity" becomes very helpful. Simply put, the more people you know, the more likely you will either be "found" for a job or business opportunity through someone's LinkedIn search, or that you can find people who can help you to network into organizations.

The bottom line: **make as many quality connections as you can**. Connect if you could see a possibility of either 1) being open to facilitating an introduction on behalf of this person, or 2) reaching out to them for an introduction.

You can manage the connection requests you receive, as well as view people in your network, by clicking on the "My Network" icon in the top menu. From this screen you can accept or "ignore" a connection request. Once you click "ignore" they won't be notified, and therefore might send you an invite to connect again. As an alternative, after clicking the "ignore" button you'll see an option to click "I don't know this person" flash at the bottom of your screen. Clicking this option will prevent you from getting invitations from this person again.

Note: if you invite people to connect who are complete strangers: They can respond by clicking on "Ignore" and then "I don't know this person" as well. If LinkedIn has received several of these "I don't know this person" clicks from your invites, they will restrict your ability to use LinkedIn!

The Exceptions to this Strategy

If you are a professional recruiter at a search firm you own, meaning your career success depends on finding the right people for positions, you may want to re-prioritize your strategy to favor quantity over quality. The reason: LinkedIn's usefulness to you may be greater as a database of potential job prospects than it will be as a pure networking tool. By connecting with the whole world, you are improving your ability to search for and find people, and communicate open positions. This benefit comes from LinkedIn enabling you to a) view the profiles of everyone in your first degree network, b) directly message up to 50 of them at a time to alert them about positions, and c) advertise positions via your Home Page Feed (see Chapter 3, page Keeping in Touch with Your Network65 for more information).

Another possible exception where you would choose quantity first before quality is if you solely want to use LinkedIn passively, to be found by other people in their searches. Then, of course, the more 1st degree connections you have, the more likely you'll come up in searches.

Here's an example of the passive approach to being found. A colleague of mine has her own wedding event planning business. In discussing her strategy, we decided that she does not need to actively "network" to get business. She just needs to be as visible as possible. So I recommended that her LinkedIn strategy involve building as large a network as possible to increase her following (see Chapter 5, page 89 for some tips on building a following). To execute this strategy, she accepts as many LinkedIn connection requests as she can, regardless of whether or not she establishes a relationship with them. This strategy is not about networking-- it's all about building visibility for her business. And it is working for her.

For many (or most) business owners (including myself), however, and all jobseekers, this passive strategy of prioritizing quantity before quality is less effective. Most business owners need a network of people they keep in touch with. This network is there for mutual support. LinkedIn excels at helping you generate and maintain this type of quality network. So my advice: unless you are one of the exceptions just discussed, don't squander this opportunity to build and maintain a great network. Prioritize quality over quantity.

For jobseekers, the approach that works best is an **active** one. That is, you don't want to be out there in the ocean, just drifting with the currents hoping they'll take you to the island of your dreams. You want to actively find the island you want to swim to, and then swim to it! That means building your network, reaching out to people you don't know, getting meetings, and keeping in touch. LinkedIn is just a wonderful tool for this active approach, Prioritizing quality over quantity improves LinkedIn's effectiveness for this kind of active career management.

Inviting Others to Connect
First select "My Network" from the top menu. You will be presented with options for how to add contacts. The fastest option for building your network quickly is by importing your address book into LinkedIn via the "Add personal contacts" panel on the left.

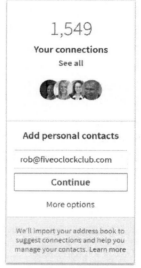

1,549

Your connections
See all

Add personal contacts

rob@fiveoclockclub.com

Continue

More options

We'll import your address book to suggest connections and help you manage your contacts. Learn more

An alternate, slower way to build your network is by sending invitations one at a time. When you send invitations, ideally you would want to personalize the invite, beyond just the standard boilerplate text that LinkedIn gives you. In particular, if the person might not remember you, remind her/him how you know each other. You can quickly find people to send invitations to individually in two ways:

1. After clicking "My Network," scroll down below "Invitations" until you see "People You May Know." You will see pages of suggestions based on the organizations and schools (and the associated time-frames) that you have listed on your profile. Having a complete list of organizations with the right spelling will help LinkedIn suggest people who may know to you.

2. Search the name of someone you want to connect with in the search box at the top of any page.

Then select her or his name and the profile will come up. You can then scroll below their picture and click on "Connect."

Note, when you find someone's profile and click the Connect button, you are "usually" able to send a brief message. The exception: when you see them as part of your search results, and then click the "connect" button right from those results. For example, when scrolling through the lists of people that come up using "People You May Know," if you click connect you will not be able to send a personal message. To send a personal message, go to their profile first and click the "connect" button from there.

Accepting Requests to Connect

When someone sends a request to you to connect, you will receive a LinkedIn notification in your email about it. You will also see the connection request under the "Network" tab in the top menu.

If you get a request from someone you don't want to connect with, I recommend that you literally just ignore the invite. If you are being bothered by repeated invitations, you could click "Ignore" and then select "I don't know this person" when this messages flashes on the bottom of your screen.

If you click this "Don't Know" option, you'll be prevented from getting invites from this person again. Keep in mind that clicking it **may cause problems for the person sending the invite**; too many of these responses will result in his or her account being automatically restricted.

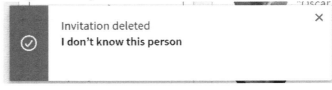

Downloading Your Connections

You can export all your 1st degree connections into a ".csv" file. The file contains your connections' name, email addresses, title and company name, and can be opened in Excel or imported into most address books (e.g. Gmail, Outlook, etc.). If you want to get your connections into your contact management system, send a mass email to all of them, or simply back up your network, this is a way to do it.

Unfortunately, this functionality is limited because you can't export only a select group of your connections. With LinkedIn, you just get one file containing all your connections, with no practical way to segment the file.

From LinkedIn's help screen, here's how you do it:

1. Click the **My Network** icon at the top of your LinkedIn homepage.
2. Click **Your connections** on the left rail.
3. Click **Manage synced and imported contacts** near the top right of the page.
4. Under **Advanced actions** on the right rail, click **Export contacts**.

To get a full archive of all your LinkedIn activity since you joined, go to the "Me" menu option, then "Settings and Privacy," then from the "Account" tab scroll down to "Getting an archive of your data."

Join LinkedIn Groups

LinkedIn groups help you connect with people you may not know to build new professional relationships and learn from group discussions. Joining groups also greatly amplifies the power of your network; you are more likely to be found by someone in need of your services.

You can also message anyone in a group that you share. The 2,000-character limit for these messages should be adequate for anything you need to share, including pitching yourself. You can search for people in your groups who are in companies or jobs in which you are interested, and then message them through LinkedIn. Note: LinkedIn limits the number of 1-to-1 group messages that you can send to 15 per month (in practice that's usually not much of a restriction).

Which Groups to Join

Join groups that have at least one of the following features:

✓ A large number of members that comprise your target audience. For example, for a client who did film scoring, this meant joining groups of Directors and Producers who might be interested in hiring him (and not necessarily a group of Film-scoring colleagues). For a typical jobseeker, it means joining groups

---

where at least half the people are employed and in a senior-enough position to hire you.

✓ Active, thoughtful discussions about topics relating to your target audience.

✓ Members who theoretically could be in a position to hire you.

Although some groups are well moderated and prevent people from posting annoying personal sales pitches, others may have no moderation at all. Many of these groups do not feature meaningful discussions. Still, even these un-moderated groups can be valuable if the members work in the places that interest you, because **you can message them via LinkedIn**.

LinkedIn hosts two types of groups, "Standard" and "Unlisted." Only Standard groups will show up in your LinkedIn search results. You may want to join certain Unlisted groups as well; to find and join these groups, you would have to either a) be invited by the group manager or b) find the URL for the group on the website of the organization or association to which you belong (alumni association groups are increasingly moving towards unlisted status).

You can search for Standard groups by going to "Advanced Search": First click in the search box, then click on the magnifying glass that appears:

Now you're in Advanced Search. Select "Groups" from the resulting menu options.

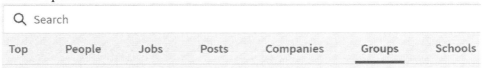

Say your job target involves Project Management. Simply select Groups from the Advanced Search menu, then enter "Project Management" in the search box. You'll see many relevant groups appear.

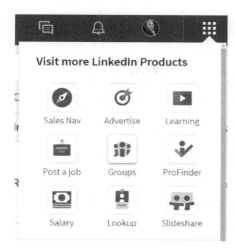

Alternatively, you can let LinkedIn suggest groups based on what's in your profile. To do this, select the Work "grid" icon in the top menu, and then pick "Groups" from the resulting options. You'll see three options worth checking out. On the main page, you'll see a LinkedIn-curated list of conversations from groups in which you already belong. On the top left, you'll see two more options, "My Groups" where you can see all your groups, and "Discover" where LinkedIn will recommend groups to you.

To find groups to join:

- Look at associations to which you already belong, such as your alumni or professional association, as they may have LinkedIn groups. For example, groups I've joined whose real-world associations I belong to include the Association for Talent Development, the Fordham University Alumni Group and the Marketing Executives Networking Group. The Five O'Clock Club has a great LinkedIn group for members, but it is unlisted—you have to become a Club member and then get invited in.
- Check for groups involving organizations where you currently or previously worked. For example, I'm a member of both the JP Morgan Chase and American Express alumni LinkedIn groups.
- Check out the profiles of people you want to meet or whose careers you want to emulate. See what groups they have listed on their profile.
- Try trial-and-error. Join a group that looks interesting by its title, description and number of members. If you're subsequently not impressed by the group conversations, you can always leave.

If you click "join" to join a group, your request has to be approved. For Standard groups, the group manager can approve your request. Also, any group member can invite you to join the group and then approve your request to join. To get approved by a moderator, often you simply need to have the right keywords in your Profile. For example, someone joining the Binghamton Alumni group would need to have Binghamton listed in the Education section. Sometimes, though, the approval process is more involved.

When you click on a group that you have joined, you will see group "Conversations" on the main screen. You will also see the number of members listed by the name of the group, as pictured.

Click on this number, and you will be able to search all group members. Once you've found a group member that you're seeking, hover over their name and click "Message" to send them a message of up to 2,000 characters. As mentioned, if you share a group with a member, you don't have to be a 1st degree connection to message them for free. They can be out of your network.

Another noteworthy menu option includes "Jobs." These are posted by group members and are different from LinkedIn "Jobs" accessed from the menu at the top of any page.

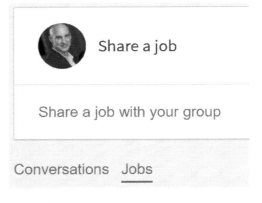

A word about Unlisted groups: if you're in a larger organization and want to collaborate virtually with just a small group of people, the ability to form such a private, unlisted group can be highly useful. I've expanded on the utility of Unlisted groups in the "For Your Business or Current Job" chapter on page 88.

Editing a group's settings

Click My Groups from the Groups main screen (or click the "Gear" icon on the top right of the page) and you will see a list of all your groups. Select the "gear" icon next to one of them and you will be able to edit its settings, including whether the group is visible on your profile and how often you get emailed about group discussions.

Also under this group settings section is the ability to search discussions by keyword, which could be useful if you're either conducting research or searching for conversations where you can contribute based on your expertise. Access this search ability by selecting "Search" from the menu.

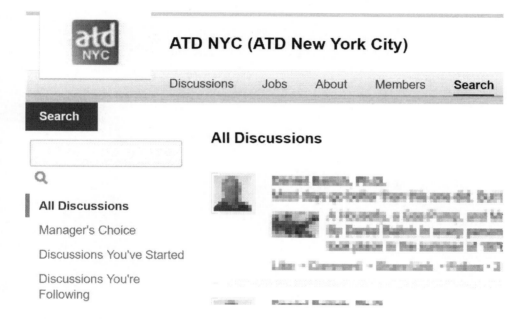

Backing Up All Your LinkedIn Data
LinkedIn makes periodic changes to their platform. Usually these changes result in improvements, but since these changes are out of your control, it's always a good idea to back-up your LinkedIn information.

Fortunately, LinkedIn gives you an easy way to download onto your computer virtually all of your activity since you joined. This backup archive includes your network, your recommendations, your profile content, profile tags or notes, messages, and of course your profile content. The full details of what is backed up and how to request the archive can be viewed on LinkedIn "help" at https://www.linkedin.com/help/linkedin/answer/50191 . Or simply go to the "Me" menu option, click "Privacy and Settings," and under the Account Tab scroll down to "Getting an archive…"

If you want to save multiple versions of your profile to, for example, revert to a prior version, a much more practical way to back up your profile is to simply export it to a pdf file. You can do this easily by clicking on the three dots to the right of your profile picture and selecting the export option.

3. USING LINKEDIN

In this Chapter:

Now that you've created your profile, begun building your network, and joined groups, you are ready to start using LinkedIn's powerful career advancement, job-search and business-building features. We'll cover the following capabilities:

- ✓ Research for job-search, business, or career
- ✓ Finding people in organizations or industries
- ✓ How to contact the people you find
- ✓ Answering LinkedIn job postings
- ✓ Keeping in touch with your network

Research for Job-search, Business or Career

For this section, we'll explore ways that LinkedIn can help you with:

- LinkedIn's new salary research tool
- Developing your target list of companies
- Viewing profiles for pre-meeting preparation
- Posing questions to your network
- Keeping current with developments in your target industries or professions

Additional research ideas with a more targeted appeal are shared in the chapters 4 ("For Your Job Search") and 5 ("For Your Business or Current Job").

New Salary Research Tool

LinkedIn has a great tool that jobseekers, recruiters and hiring managers can use to estimate compensation (salary plus bonus and equity) by profession, region, education, experience level and company size. LinkedIn will also show you the locations for the highest salaries given the job title and industry you have selected.

To access it, click on the "Work" Grid icon on the top menu, and select "Salary." The data is expected to be rolled out globally by the end of 2017.

If you have a free LinkedIn account, you need to give anonymous salary information for a prior position to gain access to these aggregated, self-reported salaries of others.

From my own research and initial client experiences, it's accuracy compares favorably with well-known salary research sites like Glassdoor.com (although this tool doesn't provide company-specific salary information like Glassdoor does). LinkedIn has done a good job standardizing job titles (e.g. it translates "office ninja" into administrative assistant) to improve accuracy.

On the other hand, there's been some anecdotal evidence that all crowdsourced salary websites may inflate actual salaries a little bit. A back of the envelop comparison in a few fields, done by a compensation consultant, shows an inflation rate of between 11 percent and 20 percent (read more at https://www.linkedin.com/pulse/linkedin-salary-calculator-launched-david-weaver). So keep this salary-inflation possibility in mind when using the site for research.

Improve Your Feed
On the "Home" page you will see LinkedIn's feed containing postings from your network and updates from people and companies that you follow. To get relevant articles published on LinkedIn by LinkedIn "Influencers" click on "Improve My Feed" by clicking on the three dots on the top right of any feed posting. You will see hundreds of LinkedIn Influencers to follow, organized by subject matter, including many well-known names. For example, I follow Bill Gates among others in my feed.

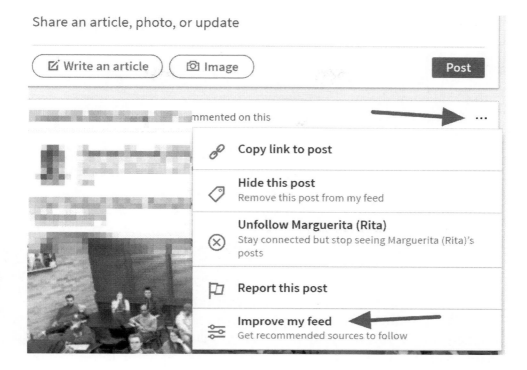

Develop Your Target List of Organizations

One of the foundations of a productive job search or business expansion involves developing a plan to market yourself, including a list of the organizations that you want to pursue. This way you are being proactive in getting what you want, and not just waiting for the ad to show up or the prospect to call.

To develop your list, use a combination of:

- Creating a list of companies (free and paid features)
- company "Insights" from within a company page
- advanced people searches
- alumni searches

Let's look at how you would go about using each of these features.

Create a List of Companies (Free Feature)

You can use Advanced People Searches to get a good start on a list of companies to target. For example, Nina was interested in working at a Hedge Fund specializing in "Alternative Investments" in the greater

Boston area but she had no idea which firms to target. Here are the steps she took.

a) She did an advanced people search. In the "keywords" text box at the top she entered "alternative investments" in quotes.
b) In the Industries filter at right she selected "investment management."
c) In the Locations filter she selected "greater Boston area."
d) She ran this search for her 1st, 2nd, and 3rd + degree network, and got a couple of thousand connections. The companies in which they work were listed by their names.
e) She refined her initial search by excluding 3rd + degree, and got a much more manageable list of under 200 names and associated companies.

Create a List of Companies (Paid Feature)

LinkedIn's premium "Sales Navigator" platform has sophisticated company search abilities which can give you a more precise and easily accessible list of companies. If you want to go beyond the free company list approach just covered and improve your list, you may want to consider a free one month trial of Sales Navigator, or pay for one month (roughly $70).

With Sales Navigator, company search abilities include filtering by keywords in a LinkedIn "Company Page," industry, number of employees, region, headcount growth, revenue, department size, how closely you're connected to people in the company, Fortune ranking, number of followers on LinkedIn and job opportunities.

Let's revisit Nina's "alternative investments" company list goal again, but this time use Sales Navigator. Here's what we did:

1) We selected "Accounts" to begin searching, and as you can see from the picture that follows, almost 12 million organizations came up.

2) We entered the keywords "alternative investments" in the left column.

3) We selected Greater Boston Area (a zip code option is also available).

4) Industry: Investment Management (which includes hedge funds),

5) Company size: we eliminated companies with a staff of 10 or less.

6) The resulting list of 135 firms was exactly what my client wanted. Not only did this list give my client the companies for her marketing plan, it also suggested people in her network to whom she could reach out for each company.

Company "Pages"

Now back to "free" LinkedIn. Another client used the Advanced Company Search feature in a different way. He was interested in the Pharmaceutical industry, in particular Pfizer and its competitors. But he didn't know who its competitors were. Here's what he did:

1) He did an advanced company search by clicking in the search box at the top, then clicking the magnifying glass, selecting the "Companies" search option and then typing in "Pfizer."

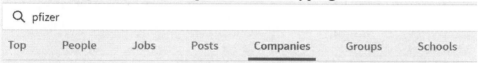

2) He selected Pfizer from the results, and was now on Pfizer's "Company Page." On the right column of the "Home" page, he found what he was looking for. He saw a section called "Similar Companies." Six were listed (here are three of them). This section gave him a list of Pfizer's competitors, which he could consider for his marketing plan.

Use Company Pages as well to research topics of interest to the people with whom you want to meet (or interview with). For example, you can view:

- A high-level summary of the company.
- Everyone in your extended network who works or worked there.

- A news feed about their company or issues in which the company cares about.
- Company offices and locations.
- Careers- job openings.

You can follow a company and receive notifications of company profile changes, news feed updates, job postings, and so forth.

Find the Right Companies in a Specific Location

Advanced People Searches are great for finding specific people to whom you can reach out. Using it for this purpose will be covered in detail in a later section. In this section, however, I want to highlight how it can be used to find companies in a new geographic area.

For example, one of my clients was a "Peoplesoft" programmer (this is a software package that is used by many HR departments). He was contemplating a move from New York to Philadelphia, but didn't know which companies (if any) in the area might hire people with his skill. Here's what we did to find out.

1) He got to the advanced people search screen by clicking on the search box at the top of any page, then clicked on the magnifying glass. He then chose "People" from the advanced search options.

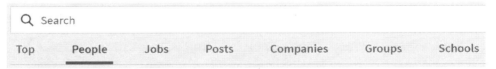

2) For the "Title" text box under the "Keywords" dropdown menu item, we entered "Peoplesoft."
3) For the "Locations" option, we selected "Greater Philadelphia Area" by beginning to type in "Philadelphia" and then selecting this item from the resulting options.
4) After clicking "Search" we found a list of people with "PeopleSoft" in their job titles, and the names of the companies at which they worked. Companies included Canon, Toll Brothers, ADP, Vanguard, Conde Nast, and many more.

My client now had a company list that he could use for his outreach, and a list of people at those companies whom he could contact.

Find companies that people went to after leaving your company

If you want to make a move to another company, or find companies to market your services to that have some relationship to companies you've already worked with, try this out. Make a list of target companies by using LinkedIn to figure out where people tend to go to when leaving their company.

For a job-search client, we used this approach, thinking that these companies would be more open to my client's candidacy since they've hired other former employees of her current employer. Plus, she might be able to get informational meetings with these ex-employees of her current company ("I see you that you used to work at my company. How are things over there at <target company>?").

Let's use IBM as an example of her current company to see what she did to create this company list:

1) She selected "People" from the advanced-search options screen.
2) In the advanced people search filters on the right she selected:
   a. Company "NOT IBM"
   b. Past Company "IBM"
3) When she ran her search, she now saw that LinkedIn gave her the top five companies that people who used to work at IBM now worked at, as part of a new list of search filters. As you can see from the picture, these companies included Accenture, Oracle, SAP, Microsoft and Google.
4) She also saw these and other companies named in her people search results on the left side.

Company

NOT IBM

School

Locations

Current companies

☐ Accenture

☐ Oracle

☐ SAP

☐ Microsoft

☐ Google

　+ Add

Past companies

☑ IBM

View Profiles for pre-Meeting Research

This ability to view profiles of people you may be meeting, or may want to meet, is a fundamental value that LinkedIn provides. For example, at one time I wanted to transition my career from the financial services sector to higher education. One person I wanted to meet, the number two person at an Ivy League school, had a LinkedIn profile that showed he himself had transitioned from financial services to higher education many years prior. I used this knowledge as a way of approaching him, relating his situation earlier in life to my current one. For this reason and a variety of others, I was able to get the meeting with him that I sought.

Pose Questions to Your Network

You can send a message via LinkedIn to anyone in your 1st degree network. For example, you might:

- Pose a question pertaining to expertise in a particular profession or industry. A client asked a segment of her network about the best blogs and resources for the advertising industry.
- Ask about hiring needs for your firm or department, e.g. "Can anyone recommend a top-notch programmer…"
- Let a certain segment of your client base or prospects know about an upcoming free webinar that you are delivering.

Search for Posts

You can also search for posts by selecting "posts" and entering keywords. Many posters make use of LinkedIn hashtags that are clickable and searchable. So you may want to try searching using these hashtags. You can also use quotes to find exact phrases, and boolean search strings such as AND, OR, NOT (these need to be capitalized) and parenthesis, as shown in the #Marketing example that follows.

Q #marketing NOT (#storytelling OR #CustomerSuccess)						
Top	People	Jobs	Posts	Companies	Groups	Schools

Find People in Organizations/Industries

LinkedIn is a fantastic tool for finding the "right" people to whom you want to reach out. We'll cover several methods in detail for finding contact opportunities:

- LinkedIn Companies
- LinkedIn Alumni
- LinkedIn Groups
- Advanced People Search
- Searching a 1st Degree Connection's contacts

Finding Contacts via LinkedIn "Companies"

Use this feature as another way to see with whom you are connected in your target companies, to ensure that you didn't miss any potential contact opportunities. Select "Interests" from the top menu, then "Companies" from the dropdown menu. Then enter the name of the company in which you are interested. For example, when I type "IBM," it gives me:

- A high-level summary of the company.
- Everyone in my extended network who works, or has worked, there.
- A news feed about their company or issues in which the company cares about.
- Company offices and locations.
- Careers: job openings at IBM.

You can **follow** a company by clicking the button; you'll receive notifications of company profile changes, news feed updates, job postings, and so forth. In the company search box, specify industry or other criteria to develop a target list of companies.

Follow

Finding Contacts Using the "Alumni" Feature

Alumni are potentially a great source for informational meetings that could lead to interviews. LinkedIn has a feature that simplifies the process of figuring out to which of your alumni you want to reach out. Go to www.linkedin.com/alumni or search for the school and then click "Alumni" on the school's page.

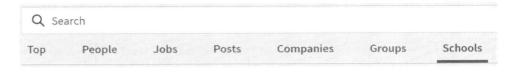

You will then see a list of your alumni and how you are connected to them, for one of the schools listed in your profile. Even more useful, your alumni are categorized by company, profession and region. Click on one of the categories for a targeted list of alumni. You can select alumni by the year they graduated (if you are targeting more senior positions, perhaps eliminate recent grads). You will also see an option to change the school, to view schools that you didn't even attend!

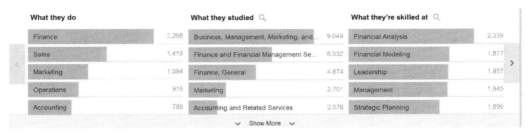

Also see the LinkedIn Alumni section under "Researching Career Options in Chapter 4, page 71 to learn about additional value that this feature provides.

Group Discussions

Use groups (see "Join LinkedIn Groups" in Chapter 2, page 39) to learn how you can help potential/current employers or clients, and to interact with people with whom you may want to connect. You can gain valuable insight from the postings of professionals in your field.

In addition, LinkedIn groups have a feature that allows you to click on "Follow This Discussion" or "Follow John Doe," so when a new post is added to the discussion, or when John posts something new, you will be alerted via email. This feature makes it easier to keep track of group discussions and people that you want to contact or learn from.

For those groups where there are active, thoughtful discussions, you may want to be notified daily by email regarding new discussion activity. You can set your preferences for group email notifications by clicking on *"Privacy & Settings,"* then *"Communications"* on the left, and finally *"Set the frequency of emails."*

Use "Advanced People Search"

Now that you have started to build up your network and you have joined groups, you can use LinkedIn's powerful "advanced people search" feature to find people to contact. Once you identify the appropriate people, either contact them directly or get introduced through your network.

To demonstrate, I'll share an example of a client, Sarah, who was interested in a marketing manager or director position at Pfizer, in or near New York City. Here's what my client did:

1. She selected the "People" option after getting to the advanced search screen.

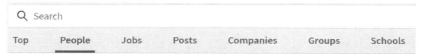

2. Under "Location," she selected "Greater New York City."
3. Under "Connections" she checked 1st, 2nd and 3rd+ degree, i.e. all LinkedIn members.

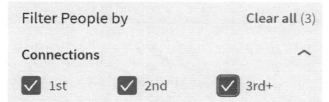

4. She clicked the Keywords dropdown menu, and under "Company," she entered "Pfizer." Note: Sarah could also have used the "Industries" menu option, instead of "Company," and selected Pharmaceuticals, if she wanted a broader industry search.
5. She then clicked on "Search" at the bottom.

Her result: Thousands of entries came up. Within the first couple of pages she saw many 2nd degree connections (people who her 1st degree contacts could introduce her to) working at Pfizer. But she realized she was not getting enough senior marketing people in her results-- that is, people in a position to hire her. So she refined her search by clicking on the Keywords dropdown menu and entering in the "Title" field:

Marketing AND (Senior OR VP OR SVP OR Executive OR Chief OR "Vice President") NOT "Senior Manager"

This character string employs Boolean logic connectors such as "AND" , "OR" , "NOT" (these need to be capitalized) and parentheses to get her the more senior level marketing professionals that she was looking for. She also used quotations so that LinkedIn would search for the entire phrase "Senior Manager" rather than "Senior" or "Manager."

The result: my client found the potential hiring managers at Pfizer that she was looking for, including a Senior Vice President- Marketing, Senior Director/Group Leader- Consumer Marketing, and a VP - Head of Global Marketing & Brand Strategy. The first two of these were 2nd degree connections, and she shared a group with the third one. She could reach out to this "group only" contact by messaging him directly through LinkedIn.

For those of you who have your own business or are looking to advance in your current role, I'm sure it's not a stretch for you to see how to apply this same approach to your own outreach.

People searches using the paid "Sales Navigator" platform: Try the "free" search I've been describing first. If that's not working for you, consider the premium Sales Navigator platform which has far more filters. Examples include being able to search by group (even if you're not a member), seniority (but you can estimate seniority on "Free" LinkedIn using the title field, as I've just shown), company type, and far more.

Also, with Sales Navigator, you can search the networks of specific individuals. For example, say someone offers to help you by connecting you to people in their network. You can't search their networks efficiently using "free" LinkedIn (you can only scroll through all of their connections, which isn't practical given the hundreds or more that people typically have and the limited visibility of individual profile information as you scroll through). You can, however, do finely tuned searches of their network in Sales Navigator.

If a Search Result lists only the Last Name's initial

If the person is a third degree or group-only contact, then you will usually only see the first initial of the last name (unless you have a paid subscription). To find the full name, try using Google—which is a back-door to additional information that LinkedIn may restrict if you search in LinkedIn itself.

For example, say your advanced people search reveals "Robert H." and the headline says: "Career & Executive Coach, Speaker | Advanced LinkedIn • Hiring • Job Search • PEAK Presentations • DiSC Team Assessments." In a case like this, not only are you restricted from seeing the full name, but you will also not be able to view the full profile.

Now, go to Google and copy the headline after typing in "LinkedIn" and the first name, e.g. "LinkedIn Robert Career & Executive Coach, Speaker | Advanced LinkedIn • Hiring • Job Search • PEAK Presentations • DiSC Team Assessments." Most of the time you will see the full name and link to the profile in Google's search results. When you click on the link in Google, you will also see the full profile!

Another approach: if the contact is from a shared group, you can also try entering the information you do have in a group-members-search; the result should show you the full name.

Be Aware of the "Commercial Use Limit"

For free, "Jobseeker-premium" and "Business-plus" subscriptions, LinkedIn will restrict the number of searches one can conduct within a given month. They don't publish the number of searches allowed, but ad-hoc testing indicates that searches need to number in the hundreds before the limit is reached. Once you have hit 70% of your search quota for the month, you will receive a warning on LinkedIn. Searches counting against the limit include any searches for profiles (except searches by name), and profile searches using the "People Also Viewed" feature that shows up on the right side of the profile you're viewing.

Based on jobseeker and business user feedback, most users will not be affected by this limit. Those that have been affected, from my experience, have fallen into two categories:

- Professional sourcers, e.g. recruiters or those in business development.
- Educators at universities who teach LinkedIn every day to students and alumni.

One way these professional sourcers have gotten around the search limit is to use "x-ray search" on Google, since at least 80 percent of LinkedIn profiles are indexed on Google. Searching using this method requires highly complex syntax, and its pros/cons and strategies are continuously debated and refined by practitioners. It is presently beyond the scope of this book.

Another option is to consider LinkedIn's premium "Sales Navigator" platform which doesn't have this limit. For more information on LinkedIn's search limit and premium subscriptions that avoid it, enter "Commercial Use Limit" in "Help."

How to Contact People that You Find

Practically speaking, there are five channels for contacting people you meet on LinkedIn. These are:

- ❖ Email
- ❖ Groups
- ❖ InMail
- ❖ Introductions
- ❖ Request to Connect

Let's talk about each of these channels. Note that I'm leaving out letter writing, which for most intents and purposes is not practical given the prevalence and ease of email. See my Appendix discussion on the topic for more about the pros and cons.

Email vs. Messaging through LinkedIn

LinkedIn is a wonderful tool for finding the right people to contact. Just because you've found the right people via LinkedIn, however, it doesn't mean that you have to message them through LinkedIn. In fact, in many cases you may prefer to try and email them! Everyone is comfortable with email, and is accustomed to getting messages from all sorts of people through this channel. Comfort with messages via LinkedIn is less consistent, which may result in a lower response rate.

Judge each situation on a case-by-case basis in terms of choosing to message via LinkedIn vs. email. I've included the example in the box that follows to illustrate further how to write these messages.

Messaging via a Group

If you can't find their email address, perhaps you share a group with them. If so, in most cases you can message people right through the group. Here's what you do:

1. Go to the group.
2. Click on "Members" (see arrow in picture that follows)

3. Enter their name in the search box.

You will see "Message" as one of the options when you hover over someone's name. The following is an example of a message that a client sent to a fellow group member. Note, that she could have easily sent this same message via email. This message resulted in an informational meeting which led to two referrals, and ultimately an interview (that's how it works—one thing leads to another and then another until finally you get the result you want).

.

How to Ask for an Introduction

One of LinkedIn's killer applications is its ability to leverage your "first degree network" to get introductions to your 2nd degree contacts. My clients make use of these introductions (as do I) for various reasons, including a job search, new business/career opportunities, as a recruiting tool, or just to learn from others. Here's how to write an introduction request that will help you to get you the meeting you want.

A client sent a LinkedIn message to someone she didn't know. This message resulted in a meeting and referral for an interview.

Dear Claire,

Upon seeing your name in the AFP LinkedIn Group and noticing our additional shared connection, I thought I would reach out to you; I myself have many years of experience with fundraising.

I'm currently a Director of Alumni and Event Planning at Ivy University. In the long run I am looking to transition outside of higher-ed, to a non-profit such as GoodOrg. Though not yet looking for a job, I would greatly appreciate 20 minutes of your time to gain your insight on how my experience might fit in a non-profit setting. Given my many years of experience developing successful fundraising strategies and events, perhaps I could also share with you some ideas that you would find useful for GoodOrg's efforts.

Some background: As you can see from my profile, I have over 10 years of experience in fundraising and event planning that could be useful to non-profits. Highlights include:

Pitch

- Developed an approach, working with IT, to identify most likely donors, which resulted in a 37% increase in donations following its implementation.
- Led a capital campaign last year that brought in $3 million and exceeded goals.
- Created partnerships with associations that provided new value to alumni; these partnerships were credited with substantially increasing donations.
- Planned and delivered a new alumni event that exceeded fundraising forecasts, and was so successful that it has been instituted indefinitely on an annual basis.

I would greatly value your insight regarding this hoped-for transition. Would you be available for a brief conversation, either in person or by phone?

Your 1st degree connections can introduce you to your 2nd degree connections. There are two ways to see a 2nd degree connection's connections that you have in common.

- Go to a 2nd degree connection's profile, and view the "Highlights" section near the top, just below the "Intro" section.

- In your people search results, any shared connections will appear under their name.

5 shared connections

Consider Sending the Introduction Request via Email

Just because you found the connection on LinkedIn, it doesn't mean that you need to send your introduction request via LinkedIn as well. In fact, email is often the preferred channel. The reason: we're all too familiar with our email inbox, but many people show lesser levels of comfort and responsiveness with LinkedIn messages. I've seen cases where individuals are unresponsive to LinkedIn messages, but respond immediately to an email (the reverse seems to be less true).

Therefore, I recommend that you default to using email to send your introduction request. Use LinkedIn to request the introduction only if a) you don't have your 1st degree connection's email address, or b) your 1st degree connection prefers that you request the introduction via LinkedIn.

Whether you use email or LinkedIn to request your introduction, the key points you need to include are the same.

Requesting Introductions via the LinkedIn Platform

LinkedIn says it "temporarily" does not have the ability to request introductions via the desktop platform. You can use a LinkedIn smartphone app, however, to request the introduction. Here's how you do it, as per LinkedIn's "help" screen:
1) In the smartphone app, go to the profile of a 2nd-degree connection whom you'd like to connect with.
2) Scroll down to the Highlights section.
3) Under Mutual Connections, tap See who can introduce you.
4) Pick a shared connection, and tap the Message icon next to their name to send them a request for an introduction.
5) Compose the message and tap Send message.

The Six Things to Include in Your Introduction Request

The bottom line: make it easy for your 1st degree connection to forward your meeting request. Let's take an example based on a client's situation. Ellen wanted to meet Susan, a 2nd degree connection, and she saw that John was their mutual first degree connection. Ellen's introduction request to John contained these six elements, in the sequence below:

1) Start with the reason for your message: Ellen began with *"Hi John, I see that Susan Smith is in your first-degree network. I would very much appreciate an introduction to her for a 10-minute conversation."* Note: asking for just 10 minutes makes it very easy for John to forward that connection, since everyone has 10 minutes available somewhere on their calendar. Also, note the word "appreciate." I'm amazed at how many clients forget to show gratitude when asking for something!

2) Then say why you want the meeting: *"I noticed that Susan works in alumni relations at Ivy University. Over the long term, I'm very interested in making a move into higher education. I would welcome the opportunity to get Susan's perspective on how the school is organized and where I might be able to add value down the road."*

3) If in a job search, say you won't ask for a job: Ellen took the pressure off by specifically saying she won't be asking for a job. *"In the conversation I seek, I will not be asking Susan about job openings; Rather, I'm looking to gain her insight into Ivy and possibly other institutions of higher-ed."*

4) Make the request mutually beneficial: Your first-degree connection is much more likely to pass on your request if she/he feels they are helping both you and the other person in their 1st degree network (and your intended recipient is much more likely to respond positively). *"I believe this meeting will be mutually beneficial. Given my many years of experience in fundraising, I could share with Susan some ideas that she may find useful for her efforts."*

5) Include your "pitch" about how you can help an organization: You'll generate more enthusiasm for the meeting by doing this. Ellen wrote: *"Susan may be interested to know that I have 10 years of experience in fundraising at non-profits, as is shown on my LinkedIn profile. During that time, I:*

- *Met or exceeded every annual fundraising goal for the past 10 years*
- *Planned and delivered dozens of successful events*
- *etc. ...*

6) Give your 1st degree an out. Perhaps John has sent too many introduction requests to Susan, or he is uncomfortable passing on this request for other reasons. Ellen still wants to maintain a good, respectful relationship with John! *"If you feel that it may not be appropriate to pass on this request, I totally understand. Regardless, I hope we stay in touch. Let me know if there's anything I can do for you."*

Another Thought specific to a Job Search

You might say to yourself "why bother with this message if I'm not asking for a job?" The reason is that these types of meetings give you access to the "hidden job market." By meeting with a number of the "right" people this way, and keeping in touch, you absolutely will begin to get referrals for interviews, or they'll think of you first when something opens up. I have several blog posts on the hidden job market under the "Getting Interviews" category if you want more information – see www.hellmannconsulting.com/blog for these and other posts.

Consider Contacting the Person Directly: Maybe you barely know the person in your network who can introduce you. Or, perhaps you have less than stellar confidence in how your 1st degree connection might represent you in an introduction. Or maybe time is of the essence— and this type of networking can take time! In these cases, you may want to send an email, LinkedIn Group message, or InMail directly to the person you are seeking to meet, saying in the subject line "Our shared connections on LinkedIn" or something similar.

Fully Leverage LinkedIn's Ability to Find the Right People: Use diverse LinkedIn tools including "Advanced People Searches," "Company Pages," your Groups, and LinkedIn's Alumni tool, to find people to connect with.

Making an introduction can benefit you as well. When you introduce Bob to Anne, you create an opportunity to send a networking message to Anne as part of the introduction. You can say: "and by the way, I've heard about all the things going on in your company. We should grab coffee sometime and catch up!"

If Someone Asks You for an Introduction

When someone asks you for an introduction, ask the requestor to write why it would be in their mutual interest to connect with your contact. This way, when making the introduction, you can feel confident that you are adding value for both parties in your network.

Using InMail

LinkedIn's "InMail" feature allows you to send anyone on LinkedIn a message, for a price. The fee is currently $10 per InMail, with a limit of 5 per month. If you buy a premium membership, a select number of InMails are included. So, do they work? Sometimes, but in my opinion not enough to place them above these other "free" methods. The drawback to InMail is that many people don't seem to read or respond well to them. My informal research says that this is because 1) many people are only nominally on LinkedIn, and may just ignore or delete messages from LinkedIn, and 2) InMail is usually used when there is no other way to connect with the person. Being that it's from a complete stranger and there is a fee element to it, many view InMails as spam.

That said, some people do have success with InMails. Plus, LinkedIn offers your money back if you pay for an InMail and you don't get a response. So, try it, but only if the other methods discussed here (emails, group messages, introduction requests) are not working for a person you want to contact.

Sending a "Request to Connect" Message

When you find someone's profile and click the "Connect" button, you are "usually" able to send a brief message. (The exception appears to be when you see them as part of your search results, and click the "connect" button right from those results; To send a personal message, go to their profile first, and click the "connect" button from there.) The problem with this approach in most cases, however, is the character limit of 300 for the message. This character limit does not provide the space necessary to convey all the elements you'll need (as described earlier in this section) for a positive response.

That said, in some cases this short message is all you'll need. For example, if you had an informational meeting with a potential client or hiring manager a couple of weeks ago, and all of the long emails have already been exchanged, sending a short, personal "Request to Connect" message may be an ideal way to keep yourself on their radar for opportunities that you are seeking.

Keeping in Touch with Your Network

Review your Home Page Feed
Click the Home menu option on top to review your Home Page feed. See what people in your network are up to. For example, a client looked at her feed and saw that someone she worked with four years prior, and hadn't spoken to since, had been promoted (his LinkedIn job title had changed). She sent him a congratulatory note. They exchanged emails, one thing led to another, and she ended up doing business with his department!

Review your Notifications page
Click on the Notifications Icon at the top of any page and you will see the opportunities that LinkedIn has identified for you to keep in touch with your network. Examples include work anniversaries, people who have liked or commented on one of your postings, birthdays, and those who have started new jobs.

Post updates to your feed
On your Home page, at the top of your feed, you'll see a place where you can enter status updates.

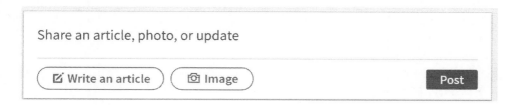

People use these updates to keep in touch with their network, as they will show up in their 1st degree connections' feed and email inbox as network updates. Being smart about posting updates means:

- Post to be helpful to others, e.g. include a link to an article that may be relevant to your network.

- Post to ask for help, e.g. mention that you're trying to fill a position in your department.

- Post to let people know what you're up to, just to keep top-of-mind with your network in case they can help.

- Try to post anywhere from once a day (or more) to no less than once a week.

Beth was looking for a senior level position in for-profit education on the West Coast. She decided to post a status update that read "Having numerous meetings on the West Coast to discuss senior level positions in for-profit education." One of her 1st degree contacts saw this update in his network updates. He contacted her and connected her with someone at an organization in which she was interested, which resulted in an interview.

Joseph was a consultant, and periodically posted helpful links that reinforced his expertise in Human Resources, particularly recruiting. Someone in his 1st degree network saw the posting and contacted him about a consulting position helping to identify candidates for a sales team.

How to Get Content for Your Posts

Feedly (a Feed Reader) can be used to quickly and easily curate information to share, by enabling you to quickly scan blogs and other sources of information. To learn more about Feedly, see Chapter 11, on Blogs. Another way to quickly scan for relevant information to share is to use "Hootsuite columns." See Chapter 10, page 110 ("Get a Social Media Manager") for more information.

LinkedIn Publisher

LinkedIn allows you to publish long form posts, essentially blog posts, for your LinkedIn audience. Click "Write an article" at the top of your Home page feed to publish a post. Everyone in your 1st degree network, as well as all of your followers, see it in their status update stream. According to LinkedIn Help:

- Your original content becomes part of your professional profile. It is displayed on the **Articles** section of your LinkedIn profile.
- It's shared with your connections and followers in their news feeds, and sometimes through notifications.
- Members that aren't in your network can follow you from your article, so that your next article will be surfaced in their feeds.
- Your article may be searchable both on and off LinkedIn, depending on your profile settings. Having your public profile visibility set to "everyone" will distribute your articles publicly.

How you use this feature depends on what your goal is. Below I've laid out scenarios for jobseekers and business-builders.

For Jobseekers: Publishing a post takes time. It's a lot of work for most of us, unless writing comes very easy and we have lots of topic ideas. For this reason, I would not advocate regularly publishing posts. That said, there are a couple of situations where you might want to occasionally publish something, e.g. just one or two posts.

- If you are making a career or industry change, or are building a new business, it's a bit harder to appear as an "insider" to your target audience; people like to hire or buy from those who "get" them. Publishing posts that resonate with your target audience can help you to attain insider status.

  For example, a client who didn't have a lot of digital marketing expertise wanted to show that he was cutting edge in his marketing job target. He published this post: "Do You Have a Social Media Marketing Plan?" He then linked to this post in his email outreach to job prospects. One employer contacted him solely on the strength of the information in this post!

- If you have been out of the job market for a long time, publishing something is a way to show that you still are current in your field. For example, an HR generalist, unemployed for a year, published a post on Federal rule changes affecting the contingent workforce. The post helped her to land the interview that got her the job offer she wanted.

For Business: Publishing can demonstrate your expertise and help you to build a following, the same way a blog can help you. In fact, I and others who own businesses will write a blog post and then publish it on LinkedIn as well, to expand the audience. On my LinkedIn profile you'll see the posts I've published.

Using Hashtags in Posts

Hashtags included in your posts (or the posts of others) are clickable and lead to search results so that you can discover other posts, and others can discover yours. Simply add a hashtag to your post (for example #funding, #jobsearch, etc.) and it will become a clickable. You can also search for a hashtag to see all public posts tagged with it.

View a Connection's Recent Activity and Highlights

If you are thinking of reaching out to someone in your 1st degree network, a shortcut to an excuse for contacting them is the "**View Recent Activity**" feature. This section is near the top of their profile, below the "Highlights" section. You can view your own recent activity as well, here's mine:

Your Articles & Activity
1,975 followers

Looking for a Job? Don't Tell LinkedIn
Robert Hellmann on LinkedIn
March 4, 2017

See 23 more articles

Feedback With A Smile! :-)
Robert commented

Listen up! Try this technique to resolve work conflicts. Its helped my clients (and me as...
Robert shared

Say NO to unstructured interviews. Need team strategy & past performance q's- our webinar...
Robert shared

See all activity

You'll find a snapshot of all their recent activity, including posts by others that they have "liked" and network updates. Not only can you use what you find as a way to start a conversation, but you should check it out just prior to a meeting that you have scheduled with them.

Note, if you don't see this section on their profile, they either a) don't have any recent activity, or b) have their profile visibility set so this section isn't public.

The "Highlights" section, near the top of their profile, also can give you ideas for how to introduce yourself, as it includes connections or groups you have in common.

How to Be Found

Don't forget to read the section in Chapter 2 on page 22, "How to Be Found." Internal recruiters and prospective customers are increasingly prioritizing LinkedIn for sourcing candidates or business partners. Make sure you optimize your visibility in their people searches.

LinkedIn's Free Smartphone Apps

LinkedIn has a number of apps. The ones you should focus on are: "LinkedIn," "Groups," "Lookup," "Jobs," and "Pulse." These apps are great for when you're on the go, e.g. commuting or heading to a meeting. And in some cases, I prefer them to the website. Here's how you can make use of each of these apps:

LinkedIn

Use it primarily for two purposes:
1)   To skim through the latest updates from your network, and like/comment.
2)   To find people with whom you are about to meet. This function is especially useful as a last minute prep, including seeing what they look like so you can recognize them in the coffee shop!

This app has functionality that mimics most of the website features. I do find the desktop/website version easier to use, however, especially when trying to do advanced people searches.

Groups

Use this app to keep up with postings in the groups to which you belong. I'm finding myself using the LinkedIn Groups app a lot. In fact, I find it easier and more natural to update myself on group conversations using this smartphone app vs. relying on the website.

Lookup

This app is useful for those of you who work in a large organization (it won't help you if you are self-employed or unemployed). Lookup helps you to find and connect with the "right" people in your organization. It complements your organization's intranet by making it easy to find colleagues on LinkedIn. You can search for them based on their position, department, really anything listed in their LinkedIn profile.

Jobs

Use this app to get updates on your saved job posting searches. Note: to start and save new searches, I find the website to be much easier to work with.

This app will also suggest people you may want to connect with, sorted by company/organization, if you sync it with your smartphone's contacts. This functionality is sort of interesting, but I find the website's advanced people search and company search features far more effective; you can more easily target just the organizations and people you are most interested in.

Pulse

This app can provide nice train reading assuming you are subscribed to the feeds through Pulse that resonate. You will see articles posted in your feed, or those that are relevant to topics in which you've expressed an interest.

4. FOR JOBSEEKERS

"Choose a job you love, and you will never have to work
a day in your life."
Confucius

Let Recruiters Know You're Open

This feature alerts certain recruiters that you are open to opportunities. Only recruiters who through their organizations use the premium *LinkedIn Recruiter* platform will have access to this feature. I train recruiters on how to get the most out of this platform, so I know that they are using it as part of their candidate-sourcing strategy. When you switch this feature on, you can indicate to these recruiters the type of position you would be open to hearing more about.

To get jobseekers to feel comfortable with this feature, LinkedIn has prevented recruiters from identifying employees within their own company who use it. Your anonymity is only protected, however, up to a point. I've heard recruiters in my classes discuss how they can get a friend at another company to tell them who in their company has this feature switched on.

But is this lack of full-proof anonymity a bad thing? Not necessarily. You can always say "I'm not actively looking, I love it here, but switched it on because I'm always interested to see what's out there. You should switch it on too!" Or they may use this insight to try and keep you! Just be aware of the limitations regarding anonymity.

To use this feature, go to "Jobs" on the main menu, then scroll down to "Update career interests" under Jobs you may be interested in.

Jobs you may be interested in
Any location · Any industry · 0 to 10,000+ employees ... **Update career interests**

Then switch on "Let recruiters know you're open."

Let recruiters know you're open   On
We take steps not to show your current company that you're open, but can't guarantee complete privacy. **Learn more**

LinkedIn only leaves this switch on for 90 days after you set it, then it reverts to "off."

Researching Career Options

Let's go beyond what we've already discussed, and identify additional career options tailored specifically for jobseekers. In particular, we'll take a look at LinkedIn "Alumni," "Jobs," "Advanced People Search" and "Volunteer Marketplace."

LinkedIn "Alumni"

I work with a number of clients who are considering going back to school or are deciding what to focus on while in school. LinkedIn's "Alumni" feature has been helpful to them in understanding how different educational choices correlate with careers. Here's how to use this feature:

1) Go to www.linkedin.com/alumni

2) Choose a college or university by selecting from the menu or search option on the right. In the picture that follows, "Fordham Graduate School of Business" was automatically selected for me because it's one of the schools I attended, as per my profile.

3) You will see columns that divide alumni by where they work, what they do, and so forth. Scroll to the right until you see "What they studied" and "What they're skilled at."

4) In the example that follows, I have chosen to view the 159 profiles of people who studied "English Language and Literature" and attended Fordham's graduate business school from 1976 to 1995. Note that LinkedIn includes in this group people who studied this subject at any school listed on their profile- that is, they may not have studied this subject at Fordham.

5) Now, you can look at the profiles of these people to learn more about their career trajectory.

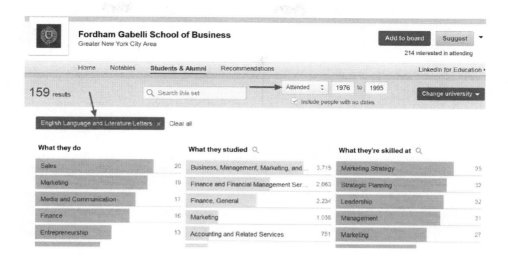

LinkedIn's "Volunteer Marketplace"

LinkedIn makes it easier to find volunteer opportunities. Gain access by going to http://volunteer.linkedin.com/ or by clicking on the "Jobs" menu option, pressing enter (i.e. searching for all jobs), and entering "volunteer" in the job title refinement filter at left. LinkedIn has partnered with some major volunteer matching sites to make this happen. This feature is great for career research, particularly if you are thinking about changing careers or industries, or are re-entering/new to the job market. Volunteering can be your ticket to the job you want, because you gain valuable experience while educating yourself on the people, job responsibilities, skills, and organizations that will be key to a successful transition. Here are a couple of client examples:

Example 1: Transitioning into a New Field

Ben had been working 50+ hours a week as an intellectual property attorney for two decades. While working full time, he was looking to make a major transition into a "community relations" leadership role at a hospital. On the surface, it seemed like a very difficult transition, given the very different knowledge and skill requirements. Here's what he did over two years:

 ✓ He volunteered his time at a community reinvestment association, eventually becoming a board member.

✓ He joined the board of another health care non-profit, eventually being elected president and recruiting a number of new members by building ties to the community.

Ben did not list this experience in the "volunteer section" of his resume and LinkedIn profile. Instead, he listed it at the very top of his professional experience (since it was as current as his attorney experience). He also highlighted his new "community relations" and "health care" experience right at the top of both his resume summary section and his corresponding LinkedIn profile summary section. He knew that the hospitals who might hire him were interested first and foremost in the experience he had that would enable him to help them, NOT whether he was paid for this experience!

Ben also made sure to use the language and keywords of the job he was going for, not his last job. This means that Ben de-emphasized his expertise in Intellectual Property, since this experience wasn't relevant for his job target. Instead, he emphasized his ability to build relationships and serve in leadership roles.

Ben's transition was hard, in the sense that he had to manage his volunteer responsibilities on top of his full-time job. But ultimately, the two years of extra work paid off; he found the career he was seeking, and the much greater job and life satisfaction that came along with it.

Lessons learned:
- Consider putting volunteer experience on top of your resume and LinkedIn profile, highlighting the experience in both the summary section and in the chronological section.
- You don't need to advertise that it was "volunteer experience," i.e. that you weren't paid for it. That is, don't diminish what may be highly valuable, relevant experience by labeling it "volunteer."
- Emphasize the skills that are attractive to your job target, de-emphasize those that aren't.

Example 2: Re-entering the workforce after years of absence
Sarah, an accountant, had dropped out of the work-force for 10 years to raise a family. Now she was ready to jump back in. But in her initial forays into the job market, hiring managers were skipping over her

profile and resume in favor of candidates who had more current experience.

Sarah filled that gap by joining a non-profit as a volunteer accountant. She immediately listed this new, highly relevant position at the top of her resume and LinkedIn profile. And importantly, she made use of the summary section, where she pitched herself as the consummate accountant, further diminishing the significance of the gap in her profile and resume. By the way, the ties she made in this organization led her to the full time job she was seeking.

Additional Lessons learned:
- Volunteer assignments can fill a gap in your LinkedIn profile and resume, making you appear more current.
- The relationships you build in your volunteer assignments can land you your next position.

See Where Former Colleagues Went

Using Advanced People Search criteria, you can find the top companies that people in your company leave for. Here's an example using IBM.

1) In the search options at the top, just below the search box, select "People."
2) In the advanced search filters on the right select:
   a. Company "NOT IBM"
   b. Past Company "IBM"
3) When I ran this search, I saw the top five companies that people who used to work at IBM now worked at, as part of a new list of search filters. As you can see from the picture, these companies included Accenture, Oracle, SAP, Microsoft and Google.
4) I also saw these and other companies listed in the people search results on the left side.

You can then refine these search results further, for example by adding keywords in the Title

Company

NOT IBM

School

Locations

Current companies

☐ Accenture

☐ Oracle

☐ SAP

☐ Microsoft

☐ Google

+ Add

Past companies

☑ IBM

field or the search box at the top to select for people who are in your field. Not only do you get more information about possible companies to target, but you now have a nice lead-in for an introductory message, e.g. *"I see you used to work at Pfizer as a Finance Director. I'm still there, am a Finance Director myself, and am wondering how things compare..."*

Use this list to help develop your job search marketing plan.

Answering LinkedIn Job Postings

LinkedIn has a powerful feature for answering job postings. It tells you who in your network is connected to the company, and in some cases who posted the position. Here is how you take advantage of this feature.

1. Click on "Jobs" on the top menu.
2. I like to get right to the advanced search filters by clicking in the jobs search box but leaving it blank, then clicking "search."
3. Now you can fine tune your search using the filters at the right, including location, company date posted, experience level, industry and job function. You can also add keywords in the text box at the top.
4. Pick one of the numerous job postings that show up. You'll right under the posting title if any of your connections work there.

   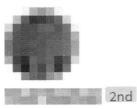 5 connections work here

5. Click on the job posting itself and sometimes you will see the ability to contact the person who posted the job, either directly or by getting an introduction if they are a 2nd degree connection.

   Contact the job poster

   2nd
   Executive Recruiter at The Evan…
   Greater Chicago Area

Use these LinkedIn features to substantially improve your odds of getting an interview; that is, don't just respond to the posting. Reach out directly to the hiring manager.

In one case, a client answered an ad, and then contacted the hiring manager directly via LinkedIn. The hiring manager called her the next day for an interview. The hiring manager had actually stopped looking at the ad responses (there were too many), and was close to making an offer to someone. But my client's message was so compelling that she had to interview her.

Some organizations will give you the option to "Apply with LinkedIn" which involves simply clicking on a button, and submitting your LinkedIn profile along with the application. The question is, should you use this feature, or apply the old-fashioned way, with a resume and a cover letter?

The answer depends largely on how close a match your LinkedIn profile is for the position. As discussed in Chapter 2, page 18, "Differences Between Resumes and Profiles," you can only have one LinkedIn profile, but you can and should have multiple versions of your resume (at least one for each job target). For many jobseekers, the LinkedIn profile will not be customized enough for the job to warrant applying in this way. But for those whose profile is a close match for the position, it is definitely an option.

You can also save searches for job postings and create search alerts, to get notified if new postings open up based on the search criteria you set. Just click on "Create search alert" to the right of your posting search results.

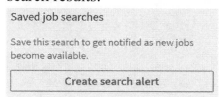

How to Prioritize LinkedIn for Your Search

Any social activity that you participate in has the potential to help you get interviews, but obviously, some are far more effective than others. One client was spending much of his job-search time going to regular networking meetings at an association where most of the people showing up were unemployed competitors for jobs in his field! It took him about two hours of commuting time to get to and from these meetings. After three months with no success, he came to me, and we mapped out more effective ways for him to spend his valuable job-search time.

A golden rule: *pick the low-hanging fruit first.* That is, do the easy things that are likely to get great results quickly before tackling the harder things.[1] Go for the biggest bang for the buck first. For example, what is the easiest way to research a person or company? Do a Google search to see what comes up, visit the company's website and poke around, or check out their LinkedIn profile.

Also, think about how you can tap into the so-called "hidden job market" via networking and building new relationships. You want to **prioritize efforts that will enable you to bypass the glut of applicants going through ads or recruiting firms**, as well as land interviews for positions that may not be advertised (or that you help to create). Most of my clients are getting interviews these days by both reaching out to their network and building new relationships with people who can help them (and not via answering ads and contacting recruiting firms). You should prioritize your efforts as well.

Follow These Steps

The sequence of job search steps below will show you how the social media applications covered in this book should fit into your larger job search. Feel free to adjust the recommended order for your unique situation.

---

[1] "Pareto Optimality," or the "80/20 rule," is the same idea (Google it, you will see pages of info). That is, we spend 20% of our time doing 80% of the work, and 80% of our time doing the remaining 20%. Focus your efforts on the 80% that takes only 20% of your time to do. A related concept: "the perfect is the enemy of the good."

1) **Research potential professions and industries**

   Use research to help you select the right positions to go for, or to ensure that you will be able to speak the language of your target audience. Some clients come to me after getting no results with their resume. Often, the problem is either that they are speaking the jargon of their last employer instead of their future one, or they don't have a clear job target and thus aren't speaking to any particular audience. Research is key to addressing these issues. Do as much or as little research as you need to depending on where you are in your job search. Approach your research in the following order:

   1. Start with the links on my website, www.hellmannconsulting.com , under "Industry and Occupational Research", to help you identify and speak to your target audience effectively.

   2. Search online job boards (websites containing job ads) to see what types of jobs exist, and how employers describe them. Adopt the terminology and jargon in these descriptions when approaching a prospective employer in the same job-target (industry or profession). If you need a starting place, scroll down to the list of job boards on the resources page of my website.

   3. Do Google searches on the profession or industry you are targeting, and see what comes up, e.g., articles, blogs, online journals, etc.

   4. Read the "Career Research" section in this chapter and in Chapter 3 on page 45; LinkedIn has a host of valuable career, job target, people and company research capabilities.

   5. Subscribe to online journals to easily search for information on your target-audience's needs.

   6. Talk to people who are in the field you want to enter to gain their insight and advice. Learn how good a fit you are for your targets, and how you should market yourself.

      You can find people to talk to by:

      a. Joining professional or alumni associations, and using their online member database to contact members for informational meetings.

b. Reaching out to people you already know, via email or a phone call.

c. Searching for relevant discussions on email lists (read Chapter 9, "Email Lists").

d. Asking questions and starting new discussions on these email lists.

e. Joining LinkedIn to ask questions of other members, read or participate in member discussions, and contact members for informational meetings.

f. Investigating whether Twitter can help you with additional target research (read Chapter 10, "Twitter").

2) Get the word out to your entire network about your search

The more people who know about your search, the more referrals you can get to people who may be in a position to hire you. Initially, you are building the wide end of your "getting interviews" pipeline, which you expect to lead to a far smaller number of conversations with people in a position to hire you. Here's the suggested sequence for making this happen:

1. Get set up on LinkedIn if a lot of people in your industry or profession use it. Read Chapter 3, "Using LinkedIn."

2. Make a list of your entire network (your dentist, family and friends, current and former co-workers, old professors— everyone you can think of) and let them know about your search. Contact them by the channel that is most likely to get a response, be it email, LinkedIn, Facebook, LinkedIn, or by tweeting your followers (see Chapter 10, Twitter). A good rule of thumb is to aim for 200 people.

3) Set yourself up for a productive search

That is, get set up for conducting ongoing job-related research, pursuing new networking opportunities, and building helpful relationships with people whom you don't know.

1. Join associations (including professional, industry, and alumni associations).

2. Similarly, join LinkedIn groups (read the "Join LinkedIn Groups" section of Chapter 2, "Getting Set Up").

3. Set up your LinkedIn home-page feed to receive timely posts about industry/sector developments (see the "Researching Career Options" section of Chapter 3, "Using LinkedIn").

4. Subscribe to the appropriate journals that will allow you to keep abreast of the latest developments in your field and identify people to contact. I prefer online journals because they are easier to search for the information you want.

5. Subscribe to blogs (see Chapter 11, "Blogs") that you find through referrals or articles you've read, to keep updated on both leaders in your field and developments in your job target.

6. Set up Google Alerts that enable you to keep on top of news regarding organizations that are of interest to you.[2]

7. Join email lists that are relevant to your job target.

8. Explore whether Twitter will benefit your target research and help build new interview-generating relationships. If so, then get set up properly on Twitter.

4) Take ongoing actions to build and maintain momentum
Once you have set yourself up for a productive search, take these actions.

1. Build your LinkedIn network (read "Building Your LinkedIn Network" in Chapter 2, "Getting Set Up").

2. Get introductions to people via your LinkedIn network (read Chapter 3, the "How to Contact People that You Find" section).

3. Remind your network of your search at least once a month, via the most appropriate channel, e.g. email, LinkedIn, Facebook,

---

[2] For Google alerts, here's what you do: 1) Go to news.google.com. 2) Type in search terms for a company you are interested in. 3) Once you like the results you are getting from the search terms, scroll down and click on "Create an email alert for <company name>."

Twitter, etc. (your update frequency will vary depending on the channel).

4. Contact people directly who you don't know using your associations' online databases or LinkedIn groups.

5. Read or participate in online conversations via LinkedIn or email lists you belong to (see the "Email Lists" section).

6. If Twitter works for your job target, briefly (15 minutes) review your Twitter "feeds" every one to three days to keep current with the latest news, and spot opportunities for new relationship-building.

5) Longer term, if the "low hanging fruit" from the steps above has all been picked:

1. Add to the comments on the blogs or LinkedIn articles of leaders in your field who might be helpful in getting you interviews or informational meetings.
2. Similarly, comment on the tweets of leaders in your field who you are following and seek to establish a dialogue that could lead to referrals/interviews (see Chapter 10, "Twitter").
3. If you are already on Facebook, explore Facebook "Groups" to see if any are worth joining (see Chapter 12, "Facebook").
4. If you feel the need to show that you are current in your field, consider starting your own blog (see the "Blogs" chapter) or "Publish" articles on LinkedIn.

Case Study: Using Limited Time Wisely

John was a business analyst interested in moving from Financial Services to the administrative side of a university in his area. He did not, however, know much about how universities could use his business analysis background, nor did he know anyone who worked at any of the universities he was interested in. So, did he run right to Twitter or start a blog? No! Here's what he did, in the following order:

1) **Alumni Associations:** John first used both his undergraduate and graduate school alumni network to see if anyone worked at

the universities on his list. Both schools had an easily searchable online database that allowed him to find names of people to reach out to in his job target.

He then emailed and phoned them to ask for 20-minute informational meetings to discuss a) how he might use his skills in a university setting, and b) who else they thought he should connect with. This was a highly successful approach; it enabled him to create his pitch about how he could help universities, and also gave him a couple of contact names.

2) **LinkedIn Profile:** As John gathered this initial information, he used it to revise his resume and his LinkedIn profile, to make him appear more of an "insider." John wanted to use the right keywords in his profile that would help him to be found by recruiters. Given that he was making an industry change, however, he knew that he would not be the ideal candidate for recruiters, and would have to rely even more on networking and making new connections via Direct Contact.

3) **LinkedIn Introductions:** Now that John had an effective LinkedIn profile, he looked at his LinkedIn network. John found that he had several 2nd degree contacts at universities where he wanted to work. He reached out to his 1st degree contacts to get the introductions.

When asking for introductions, John made it clear that he would not be asking for a job. Instead, he asked for a brief, mutually beneficial conversation about how his skill set could be useful to a university down the road. His introduction requests were accepted.

4) **Making new connections via LinkedIn Groups:** John also noticed a couple of contacts at universities in his target area where they shared only a common LinkedIn group. John messaged these contacts directly through the LinkedIn system. In his message, he:

    a. Made it clear he wasn't asking for a job, but rather an informational meeting.

    b. Found a way to say the meeting could be mutually beneficial.

    c. Asked for only 20 minutes of their time.

d. Included his pitch, in which he emphasized how his skills might benefit a university down the road.

5) **Updates to LinkedIn Network:** John also began keeping his LinkedIn network updated on his activities via his Home page feed. In one instance, he made a comment about how to analyze donor information to increase university fundraising opportunities, and linked to an article. One 1st degree contact who saw his post sent him this message: "I didn't know you had this kind of expertise! You should really talk to a client of mine; he would be interested in your background." This exchange resulted in an informational interview, which in turn led to an interview for a new position.

6) **Updates to his Remaining Network:** John thought broadly about his network and included his friends and family, his former colleagues from 10 years ago, and a former teacher. He surprised himself by coming up with close to 200 names!

He then contacted these 200 people to ask for their help in making contacts at universities he was focusing on. He did this in two ways. 1) He sent out a mass email to all those he had an email address for. 2) He also was very active on Facebook, so he sent the same message out to all of his Facebook "friends." John got numerous responses this way, with some very productive leads.

7) **Industry Publications:** John did a search on some online journals for articles that could give him more background on both his target universities and on people to contact. In one, the *Chronicle of Higher Education*, he found two relevant articles written by well-placed administrators in target universities.

He contacted both by email, introduced himself, referenced their respective articles, included his pitch, and requested a meeting not to ask for a job, but to have a mutually beneficial discussion. He got meetings with both of them that eventually led to interviews.

8) **Professional Association:** John joined "CASE," an association focused on university Advancement, an area he felt his business analysis expertise could help in. It cost him around $80 for the year, but was well worth the investment. He found an abundance

of articles online that gave him greater insight into how he could help potential employers.

9) **Email list:** John began participating in the CASE email list, and over time began building up additional contacts that gave him more of an insider status.

10) **Looking Like an Insider:** By now John had a robust search going on. He had many leads into the universities and colleges he was interested in. His initial conversations with alumni helped him figure out how to sell his skills to those who might be in a position to hire him in his job target. Now two months into his search, he was having six concurrent conversations with people who were in a position to hire him.

11) **Preparing for Interviews:** To prepare for his interviews John set up "Google Alerts" for the key universities he was targeting, so that he could keep on top of the latest news for his job target.[3]

12) **Experimenting with Twitter (see Chapter 10, Twitter):** John also decided to help prepare for interviews by checking out Twitter. John spent about three hours researching Twitter to see if there was any potential for him to use this platform.

First, he tried searching for Twitter users to follow. John found, however, that none of the users he uncovered were really worth following, as the tweets reflected mainly on-campus student activities. Then John went to Hootsuite and tried creating search columns for the universities he was targeting. He found that their tweets were mostly targeted to on-campus activities as well.

John ultimately created two columns on Hootsuite that did turn up relevant tweets, involving the keywords "fundraising advancement" and "university tuition". He decided, however, that it would be easier to keep track of this information by "following" these Universities on LinkedIn, to read their postings; he wouldn't have to keep opening a separate Twitter application. John decided he had spent enough time investigating

---

[3] He did this by a) going to news.google.com, doing a keyword search, then if he liked the results, scrolling to the bottom and selecting "Create an email alert."

Twitter and would rely on LinkedIn for the information he needed.

13) **Blog:** John decided to publish an article on LinkedIn, just one, to demonstrate his additional expertise in business analysis as it pertains to university Advancement. He did begin keeping track of college Advancement blogs on *Feedly* (see Chapter 11) that he found out about through the CASE email list.

14) **Tweeting:** John didn't really consider tweeting, because he felt the time was not worth the effort. He was already getting strong positive results from his other methods.

Over a three-month period, while still working full-time at his financial services job, John managed through this effort to obtain several interviews for positions he was interested in. He had to juggle multiple job offers, finally accepting an offer in which he was very interested.

John's results demonstrate how online social media can combine with more traditional approaches to create a highly successful job search. May you too achieve success in your search!

Additional Job Search Case Studies

1) Elena was interested in working at Apple Computer as a Process Improvement manager. She conducted an "Advanced People Search." She entered Apple as the company name. To her surprise and delight, she found that an old classmate she was connected to via a LinkedIn Group worked at Apple in a related area. She emailed him directly—and ended up eventually with an interview.

2) Armando was searching for a senior level position directing a marketing analytics group. He conducted an "Advanced People Search" using the word "Marketing" in the job title. He saw that he was indirectly connected to a Chief Marketing Officer through two 1st degree connections. Using the LinkedIn smartphone app he got introduced to that person through their mutual contact, and they agreed to meet. This meeting led to a series of interviews and a job offer.

3) Janis was interested in researching the field of Organizational Development. She joined a Group called the "Organizational Development Network." This Group's discussions were lively and informative. She was able to get answers to a range of questions, and contributed to the discussions where she could. New contacts she made via the Group led to several informational meetings.

4) David was in retail store sales management. He was looking to meet a senior executive in a top New York luxury retail outlet where he wanted to work. Through an advanced people search, he found the name of the person he wanted to reach. He saw in the "Highlights" section of their profile that they shared both a group and a mutual connection. David messaged this executive through the group, using the guidelines specified in the "Messaging via a Group" section of this chapter. 13 minutes later (according to his happy email to me), he received a reply agreeing to a meeting for an exploratory interview (which ultimately led to a job offer).

5) Nina was interested in working at a Hedge Fund specializing in "Alternative Investments" in the greater Boston area but she had no idea which firms to target. Here are the steps she took.

    f) She did an advanced people search. In the "keywords" text box at the top she entered "alternative investments."

    g) In the Industry filter at right she selected "investment management."

    h) In the Location filter she selected "greater Boston area." clicked on "Companies" (under "Interests") then "Search Companies."

    i) She typed "Alternative Investments" in quotes in the company search window at the top.

    j) She ran this search for just her 1st and 2nd degree connections, and got 202 people, representing roughly 100 companies.

5. FOR YOUR BUSINESS OR CURRENT JOB

Your "Company Page"

If you are a solo consultant, then a company page will have limited value. Since your "brand" is essentially you, your profile functions as both your networking tool and your "company page." While it can't hurt to create a company page, and will give you another channel for building followers, you will find that most people will follow you personally via your profile, and not your company.

If, however, you have multiple employees, are looking to actively hire, and have specific products you want to showcase, then a Company Page is definitely a good move. Company Pages allow you to:

- Build brand visibility by having your employees connect to your company page from their profiles

- Build a following outside of, and in addition to, those following your profile

- Post "Company Updates" that may be different from the updates you would post from your profile

- Showcase products and your organizational culture.

- Announce open positions and expand recruiting options

Setting up a company page is very easy. Simply click the "Work" icon on the top menu, scroll down to the bottom and you'll see "Create a Company Page." After that, just follow the instructions to fill out the page.

As you set up your LinkedIn company page, ensure that you create the ability to post updates to your page followers. To do that, in the Company Page Administration section, make sure you select "Designated Users Only" and then enter your name as the designated user.

Note: some Company Page features require a premium subscription, for example, if you want to add a "Careers" section to the company page. This section is particularly helpful in attracting top candidates; use it to help brand your organization as an employer of choice.

To see the potential of a company page, check out LinkedIn's own company page, as well as its list of the "10 best Company Pages" from its blog: http://ow.ly/L5C83.

Build a Following

Build a following by using a combination of status updates through your profile and your company page, as well as LinkedIn Publisher posts. Consistency and regularity of your posts is key to building a substantial following. Here are some Do's and Don'ts. **DO**:

- Post items of value, usually links to useful articles, discounts or advice that's really a value-add.

- Post occasional announcements of your products or events.

- Post occasional requests for help.

- Post resonant updates at least once a day, to once a week.

- Publish long-form articles (via your Home page feed) roughly once a week.

- Throw in something personal every so often—so people can relate to you—especially if your business is you!

On the other hand, **DON'T**:

- Consistently post content that very few people care about.

- Relentlessly sell through your posts.

Research for Your Business

Use LinkedIn to advance your business (or your employer's business) through competitor research, or through identifying likely prospects.

Conduct Competitor Research

To take just one example of many: A client held a senior position at a fast-growing information technology cloud services company, and wanted to see how some of his slightly larger competitors organized their IT departments. He conducted advanced people searches using criteria including the competitor company name, job title, and keywords. The result: he was able to get a sense of the number of IT positions at a particular competitor, as well as the function of each position. Using this information, he was able to make the case for moving his company's hiring strategy in a new direction.

Identify Organization Prospects

Use the organizational list building ideas that we discussed on page 47, *Develop Your Target List of Organizations*. Once you have your target list of organizations, do advanced people searches, filtering by company and title keywords, to find the right people in which to reach out.

Jack wanted to reach out to accountants with a new service his team had developed that would match potential accounting clients with the accountants who could help them. His target prospect was a small firm or sole proprietor in the New York City vicinity. Here's what he did to identify accountants for his marketing outreach, using an advanced people search.

1. Jack entered "CPA" in the company name, since he thought that a firm having this acronym in the company name would indicate a small or sole-proprietor accounting firm.
2. For Industries he selected "Accounting."
3. For Locations he selected "Greater New York City Area."
4. At first he selected 1st, 2nd and 3rd + degree connections. When he clicked "search," however, he received over 3,000 results, which was a bit too much for him to go through initially.
5. When he narrowed the search down to just his 1st and 2nd degree connections, however, he received 128 results – people who mostly were the principals in sole proprietorships or small companies. This list gave him the start he needed. Also, since the list comprised companies with people in his 1st and 2nd degree network, he thought they would be more likely to respond to his outreach.

LinkedIn's Sales Navigator Platform

This premium platform enables you to conduct and save far more sophisticated searches, of both organizations and people, than free LinkedIn. If your job is sales or business development, you may want to check this platform out, at https://business.linkedin.com/sales-solutions/sales-navigator.

Recruiting

When a position opens up in your organization and you need to hire, what's the first thing you naturally do? Think about who you might know, right? LinkedIn exponentially multiplies the power of this mental review. Just do "Advanced People Searches" using the Boolean logic described in Chapter 3, page 55, to find exactly who you are looking for. When you see someone with whom you are interested in speaking, you may not be able to tell if they are actively looking, especially if they take the advice I gave in the "Getting Set Up" section! No matter, just send them an email or InMail that says something like:

Dear Mr. Hellmann,
I found your profile on LinkedIn and thought I would reach out to you. I am the Director of Student Development at Ivy University. Your program-related experience and University affiliations are impressive! I am currently looking for a full-time staff member to develop career-related programs for students. Specific expertise in Financial Services and/or finance is a plus, as is a network of established recruiters. If you are interested, I would welcome a conversation with you. If not, I would appreciate your forwarding this note on to anyone in your network who might be interested and qualified. Thanks for your consideration.

LinkedIn Referrals

While this book focuses on mostly free features accessible to anyone, this paid platform is worth highlighting; it has the potential to greatly expand your company's ability to get quality referrals to apply for open positions (and we all know that referrals are a great channel for quality hires).

LinkedIn Referrals makes it easy for you to see who your employees know, and for employees to identify and reach out to the right connections and invite them to apply. In fact, the Referrals software will automatically email those employees who it judges can provide referrals, highlighting open positions and suggesting people in their network who they can invite to apply. You can find more on this capability here: https://business.linkedin.com/talent-solutions/employee-referrals# .

LinkedIn Recruiter

Another paid platform worth mentioning, LinkedIn Recruiter exponentially expands on the existing and already substantial free capabilities of LinkedIn (I partner with LinkedIn to teach recruiter to those who've purchased the subscription; email rob@hellmannconsulting.com if want to learn more). For example, you get:

- Far more search filters, so you can home in on just who you're looking for, including those most likely to respond
- Recruiter team-collaboration tools so you speak with a single voice and improve efficiency and effectiveness
- InMail, search and pipeline analytics that will help you to improve your response rates
- Visual insights of the base of potential hires, so that you can quickly understand options; these insights are invaluable if you're a recruiter looking to build a strategic partnership with hiring managers.
- The ability to search and view all profiles, as well as tag them, track them, and keep updated on career changes.

If your company has the budget, great, check out Recruiter.

Maintain Team Profile Consistency

At the very least, all employees should list your organization correctly in their profile, so that the organization logo (from your Company Page) is visible. Your brand's visibility will improve through this kind of interconnection. In large organizations, ensuring the correct organization listing will also help your employees, by enabling them to find each other on LinkedIn for collaboration.

For business development or sales teams, I would recommend taking this standardization a step further. Have all members of your team include one or two keyword-rich sentences in the company description that represent your company's pitch. For example, *"ACME Company operates at the cutting edge of wearable technology; we develop tools for inventory, shipping and the Logistics and Transportation Industry."* Every business development person should also "follow" your company in LinkedIn (click "Follow" on the top right of your company page), to boost your company's brand visibility.

Be careful about forcing too much standardization. Exerting too much control over an employee's LinkedIn presence can be a significant contributor to their decision to leave your organization (as a career coach, I've seen it happen too many times). In the current employment climate of job insecurity, everyone (including you) needs to maintain an active network, even when things are going great!

Concern about Making Client List Visible to Competitors

Occasionally business owners or their employees will ask me if they can hide their network from others, to protect competitors they are connected to from identifying their clients by looking at their network. You can hide your connections, but there's no ability to be selective. You either hide all your connections from everyone or no one. To do so, just go to "Privacy and Settings" and then click "Select who can see your connections," and finally choose "Only you."

While you can hide your connections from everyone, doing so could ultimately hurt you in the sense that you are not ""giving" to your network; hence you may not "get" from others. Beyond that, I don't see a compelling reason to hide your connections. If you have several hundred connections, it doesn't seem likely that your competitor will either take the time to go through them all, or be able to figure out who is a client vs. just a colleague, friend, or acquaintance. So, my recommendation is not to worry about this issue. In our interconnected world, it's so easy to get information on others regardless. And as they say, "keep your friends close and your enemies closer…"

Your Profile: for You or Your Business?

Some clients who are consultants or business owners ask me whether they should create a LinkedIn profile that reflects their company, not themselves. Usually, the answer is no. The reason: the LinkedIn profile, and the network that connects to it, is just too good of a tool for **real networking** to waste this part of LinkedIn on simply a company promotion.

Many (perhaps most) business owners benefit from an active network of relationships that have been built and maintained over time. LinkedIn excels at helping to create this kind of network. If your business is one of those that benefits from a network, then don't squander the network-building opportunity that LinkedIn provides by using your profile solely as a promotional piece. Instead, ensure that your profile works for networking. Then consider whether building a LinkedIn Company Page will allow you to create the following you are looking for.

Boost Success in Your Current Job

LinkedIn is particularly helpful in two areas that I emphasize to clients for achieving on-the-job success.

- ✓ **To find "Security" you need "Marketability"**
- ✓ **Build and Maintain a Network**

Let's look at each of these areas.

To find "Security" you need "Marketability"

To succeed on the job these days, you need to keep yourself and your skill set on the cutting edge. You have to think of yourself as a "consultant" for your current employer, always looking outside to bring in new value. Being an expert in anything seems more and more to be only a temporary situation. Things change quickly, and suddenly your expertise is obsolete or no longer needed. LinkedIn is a great tool for helping you to see what your "competition" is doing so that you can ensure you are maintaining your value and bringing in new ideas. Here are a few ways to do this:

- Research keywords that people use in your job target through advanced job-posting and people searches.
- Monitor or participate in LinkedIn Groups that have active discussions in your field.
- Leverage your LinkedIn home page feed to get topical articles about your field delivered to your inbox. Select "Improve My Feed" by clicking on the three dots on the top right of any post.
- Follow people who are leaders in your field, within LinkedIn. Just click on "Follow" under their name and picture when you see that they have posted something in a group you share, or published an article, and both your feed and your email updates will highlight their latest postings.

Build and Maintain a Network

As a career coach with 20 years of experience in the corporate world, it has become clear to me that relationships are at least 50% of career success (the other 50% being how well you can do your job). With some jobs, e.g. business development, relationships count for even more! Maintaining a quality network over time is invaluable. Your network will enable you to learn about how to be best in your profession, hear about things that that may impact your job (before it's too late), hire good people, and quickly make a move within or outside of your current organization, if necessary. Read Chapter 2, "Getting Set Up on LinkedIn to see how to create a quality network.

Here's an example of how having a quality network helped a colleague to fill an open position.

Recruiting Using Your Network

Julietta needed to hire a part-time consultant for New York University, where she was a Director. She went to "Advanced People Search" and entered keywords that related to her need, including "career services" among others. She also entered "New York University" as both a keyword and the "School," as she preferred someone who was an alum or had already done work with the school.

Near the top of her list of search results she found Marc, among others. He seemed to have the experience that she was looking for, based on the prominence of her keyword search terms on his profile. Julietta checked out Marc's several recommendations. They looked impressive, given both the content and the levels and responsibilities of the people who recommended him.

Julietta decided to reach out to him. She emailed him directly, since his email address was listed in the "Contact" section of the profile. In her note, she described the position to him, and asked if he or someone else he knew might be interested. Marc expressed his interest in the position. They met, and had a great conversation.

Julietta had noticed on LinkedIn that they had a couple of mutual first degree connections whom she knew well. Julietta reached out to these mutual connections for additional reference checks. They came back strong. Julietta also found a number of other good candidates solely from her LinkedIn outreach. Some were referrals from her LinkedIn network. She ended up hiring Marc.

Using "Advanced People Search" is a great way to see if you have anyone in your network who might be able to fill a position. You may want to check with your Human Resources department, however, as they may have a paid subscription that allows them to do more sophisticated searches.

Start an Unlisted Group

Starting an Unlisted group within your organization can be a great way to network and collaborate with others, improving productivity. For example, I founded the "Career Coach Network" members-only group for Five O'Clock Club career coaches. The group is unlisted so that discussions can be kept private, and focused on the organization's business and advancement without fear of intrusion from competitors. As an unlisted group, you would have to be invited by the group manager to be able to join, and the group does not show up in LinkedIn's search results. Access is restricted.

It is easy to set up your own LinkedIn group. Just go to "Groups" under the "Work" icon in the top menu, select "My Groups," and then "Create a Group."

Supplement Your Organization's Intranet

If you are in a large organization, LinkedIn is a great resource for finding and reaching out to others in different departments. For example, one client worked at JP Morgan Chase, a company with over 200,000 employees. He wanted to learn about a new area of the company for a possible move down the road. Using "Advanced People Search," he found the profiles of several people at Chase that he decided to reach out to via email.

In addition, LinkedIn has a smartphone app, called "LinkedIn Lookup," whose specialized purpose is to supplement your organization's intranet; it's designed to find colleagues on LinkedIn who work at the same place as you do. Using this app, you can search for internal colleagues with specialized skills, responsibilities or experience (based on what's in their profile).

LinkedIn Profinder

You can get new clients, or find vendors, using LinkedIn profinder. The platform enables members seeking a product or service to, for free, find professionals who can help them. For businesses and freelancers looking to advertise their products or services, the first 10 proposals are free. After that you will need to have a Business Plus subscription (currently $60/month) to continue to submit new proposals that advertise your services.

With Profinder, LinkedIn is competing with Upwork and similar freelancer marketplaces. One of the key differentiators, however, is that LinkedIn is not an intermediary; it doesn't accept payments, it just brings buyer and seller together.

I advocate that any business not constrained by specific compliance issues (e.g. some financial services providers) should take advantage of the 10 free proposals and try Profinder to see if it works for them in driving business. Note: to get the most out of this platform, it's imperative to have a properly positioned LinkedIn profile, including stellar recommendations!

To get started using Profinder as a buyer, click "Profinder" under the "Work" icon on the top menu, or just go directly to www.linkedin.com/profinder. If you want to sell your services, go instead to https://www.linkedin.com/profinder/pros.

6. LINKEDIN'S PAID SERVICES

LinkedIn offers packages of paid services at different price points. Since the free features in LinkedIn are already so useful for career or business advancement, don't sign up for the paid services right away. Use them if you feel you have maxed-out on LinkedIn's free features.

For the "Business Plus" and "Jobseeker Premium" packages, I'll note the more useful paid features.

- You can send a limited number of "InMails" without having to pay $10 each time. This feature allows you to message anyone in LinkedIn, whether you are connected to them or not.

- You can see the full profiles of anyone in your extended network. This feature actually can be useful if you are preparing to contact someone at an organization, or preparing for an interview. You may or may not need this; Try searching for the individuals on Google first to see if you can view more of their profile that way. See Chapter 3, page 57 for more information about how to use Google as a back-door to LinkedIn.

- You get more search results for a given search. In practice, I've found this feature to be not particularly useful, as most people scan just the first couple of pages of results regardless.

- For some premium versions, you are not subject to the Commercial Use Limit for people searches. In practice, this limit usually does not impact casual or episodic users, which includes jobseekers. It does impact "professional sourcers" like recruiters and those in business development; If you fall into this category, a premium subscription to LinkedIn's "Sales Navigator" might be the way to go. Enter "commercial use limit" in LinkedIn Help to find out more about which subscriptions can remove the limit.

- You can get an extended history of "Who's Viewed Your Profile." As mentioned previously, don't get fixated on this feature. Use it initially to figure out if the "right" people are viewing you, fine tune your profile based on this feedback, and then mostly just let it go (if people look at your profile and then don't want to contact you, don't try to force them!). Paying for this extended history has limited value.

- For the Jobseeker Premium subscription: When you answer a job posting, LinkedIn will highlight subscribers' applications, putting them at the top of the list as a "featured applicant." This sounds compelling until you take into account:

    o You will still be just one profile among a potentially large glut of paid member applications at the top.

    o Does "featured applicant" designation really help? Maybe, but I'm not so sure. Perhaps some applicant reviewers are turned off by the "ad"!

    o You have to apply through LinkedIn—that's something you may or may not want to do depending how you decide to set up your profile.

    o Answering ads should be only the smaller part of your job search effort, so perhaps limit your investment! You really need to go way beyond ads. For example, seek out and contact the hiring managers directly using the ads as a tip-off. Leverage your network and contact "strangers" directly to build relationships that can give you access to the "hidden job market." See my blog posts on this "active" approach to the job search for more information, at www.hellmannconsulting.com/blog .

- For the Jobseeker Premium subscription: When you apply for a job through LinkedIn, you can learn how you compare to others who are applying in terms of your credentials. This feature could be useful in the early part of your search. At some point, however, you will have optimized your profile and resume, and will receive diminishing returns from this comparison.

LinkedIn has additional platforms for organizations. They all require substantial annual fees, beyond the reach of most individuals. These platforms include recruiting tools such as:

- **LinkedIn Recruiter**: If your organization can afford the annual fee, it's well worth your while to try it (I know, as I teach it to recruiters).

- **LinkedIn Referrals**: This platform helps you leverage the power of your employee network to source top candidates.

For more information on these two recruiting tools, see page 91.

Another platform that has received a lot of positive feedback is **LinkedIn Sales Navigator**. At roughly $70/month, it's far less expensive than the recruiter platforms. It helps you surface and track prospects within LinkedIn, and close deals. If I had to pick one add-on to strongly consider, both for jobseekers and business-builders/consultants, it would be Sales Navigator. Benefits include:

- The ability to create precise lists of organizations for which to target, based on many different criteria.

- Dozens of additional people search filters that let you hone in on just the type of person you are looking to connect with.

- The ability to search the networks of specific people. For example, you may have a friend or colleague who has offered to help you. One of the best ways to take them up on their generous offer is to search their LinkedIn network to see if there are any people to whom you would want them to introduce you.

Although this platform is called "Sales" Navigator, I find it the most compelling of the premium offerings for jobseekers. The reason: in a job search, your "job" becomes sales since you are selling yourself! Jobseeker Premium is more reactive (i.e. helping you with job postings that show up, or people that are looking at you). Sales Navigator is all about being proactive, finding the people and organizations to whom you want to reach out. Most jobseekers these days are landing interviews using these proactive methods (getting introduced through their network or contacting "strangers" directly). If you want to learn more about tapping into this "Hidden Job Market" check out my blog www.hellmannconsulting.com/blog (select the category "Getting Interviews").

If you've maxed-out on the free features of LinkedIn, consider taking LinkedIn up on their offer of one free month of Sales Navigator (a free month may be all you need). For more information, go to: https://business.linkedin.com/sales-solutions/sales-navigator.

7. COMMON CONCERNS AND QUESTIONS ABOUT LINKEDIN

People unfamiliar with LinkedIn often raise these concerns to me. Here are my answers.

"My Boss Will Know I'm Looking"

Your boss will not see that you are asking for introductions and contacting people in groups. As far as other updates to your Profile, the mere fact that you are active on LinkedIn should not mean to your boss or anyone else that you are necessarily looking for a job. Many people (including myself) use LinkedIn to enhance success in their current positions. In addition, it is certainly advisable that everyone, your boss included, keep up with their network via LinkedIn.

That said, LinkedIn can be a challenge if you are trying to make a career change without your boss knowing. Your boss could become suspicious if your profile reflects a different profession than your current one. My advice: instead of a targeted profile that speaks just to employers in your new career, have a broader profile that encompasses both your current position and your new career direction.

For example, I had a client who was interested in moving from business- development in information technology to financial analysis. So his profile positioned himself broadly, as a "Finance and IT professional with broad experience including financial analysis, business development, and IT."

Note that I advise a more focused, targeted approach for your resume and pitch. The reason: you can only have one profile, that's visible to your entire network (you can't pick and choose, it's either your entire network or no one), while you can and should have a different resume for each job target.

Should you block your boss? Maybe. The risk is that they could find out, which could land you in hot water and even get you fired if you are violating a Company policy on LinkedIn profile content. On the other hand, if you have a crazy boss who isn't that sophisticated about LinkedIn, blocking might be the way to go.

"I don't want some people to know I'm changing my profile"

Occasionally someone asks me whether there is a way to selectively prevent certain people from being notified about profile updates. You cannot prevent notifications to select individuals, but you can prevent notifications to your entire network. See page 16, LinkedIn Settings, to see how to do this.

"I don't want all of my information out there for anyone to see"

As mentioned in the "Getting Set Up" chapter, you can alter your settings to make them visible to different groups of people, from everyone to just your 1st degree network (or to no one at all). I would advise at the very least having your profile visible to the people you connect with.

"Should I only connect with people in my profession?"

The answer is no. You never know who knows someone who knows someone. Recently a client whose job target was "financial analyst" landed a coveted interview because she had connected with her next-door neighbor, with whom she had a distant but friendly relationship. It turns out that the neighbor's husband's brother-in-law knew the CFO at a company she was targeting, and put her in touch. In fact, through both client and personal experiences, I've found that it's often the people you least expect, the ones you're more loosely connected to, that offer the most help.

8. PRIORITIZING LINKEDIN AMONG OTHER SOCIAL MEDIA

"Do first things first, and second things not at all."
Peter Drucker

Social media has a lot of buzz: What is all this twitter about Twitter? Do I really need to link-up with LinkedIn or face Facebook? In selecting applications to prioritize along with LinkedIn, I considered: 1) whether helpful career advancement features are free to use, 2) how useful these features are, 3) the number of users, and 4) the amount of media attention. These factors led me to focus on four applications:

Email Lists: are an often-overlooked, "low-tech" social networking tool. Yet they have shown great results and are widely accessible.

Twitter: has received a lot of press and has many users, including leaders in a variety of professions. It may have potential to enhance your job search or career, depending on your profession.

Facebook: With over a billion users, Facebook is just too large for it not to be evaluated.

Blogs: are easy to access and use, and have potential as a job-search aid in many situations.

On another note, I excluded platforms that, although in many cases very popular and frequently mentioned in the media, just don't yet have the usage volume, the career-oriented "culture," or are too specialized to one type of business or career-advancer and don't have the broad-based practical career applications to be included. These platforms include Google+, Pinterest, Instagram, Foursquare, and a host of smaller applications.

9. EMAIL LISTS

"I get mail; therefore I am."
Scott Adams

In this Section:
- ✓ Many associations have active, thoughtful email lists that cover hot-topics in your field. If so, you should take advantage of this important benefit.
- ✓ Search email "conversations" in list archives to learn more about your profession.
- ✓ Ask questions of other colleagues on the list that can help you with your search.
- ✓ Answer questions posed by list colleagues, to help build your reputation.

Email Lists (also referred to as electronic mailing lists, or sometimes incorrectly as *Listserves*) are a tool for sharing messages among individuals who subscribe to the list that form conversations around specific topics. These conversations can be archived and are searchable. You do not need any special software to subscribe to an email list.

These lists can be useful for any aspect of career management or building a business. Messages can be created, viewed, and replied to via your email inbox or online through the site that hosts the messages. Many of the most useful email lists are offshoots of professional associations that you already (or will) belong to, as part of your approach to getting interviews. Below are two examples from my own experience.

MENG, or the Marketing Executives Networking Group (www.mengonline.org), an organization that I belong to, has an email list set up that can be viewed from its website, or via messages received in your email inbox. There are strict rules for the types of messages that can be sent. Moderated email lists, such as this one, facilitate the most interesting, useful discussions.

One of the formats on the MENG email list allows you to start certain messages with [Requests], meaning you want to ask the members for information. I had a client who used this format to ask the membership if they knew how to approach a particular person or people at a large multinational company. This request garnered many responses, one of which led to an interview.

The second example: the Organizational Development Network (ODN) (www.odnetwork.org) has a very active email list with professionals who are devoted in helping each other to advance in their careers and share learning. To give you an idea of the quality of the discussions on a good email list, I went to the ODN's website and skimmed the most recent archives, and immediately saw substantial discussions on the following topics:
- What OD Blogs do you read?
- Distinguishing between OD and Training
- HR and OD

Hopefully you are seeing how participating in email lists like these can help you. They enable learning by reading the discussions, asking questions, and contributing your own valuable comments and insights, which will serve to impress prospective employers. They also help you to build relationships that can lead to referrals for meetings or interviews.

Note: Before posting on an email list, observe the etiquette of the posts and use a similar style yourself. In addition, if you can, be proactive in answering your colleagues' questions. This is an effective way to market yourself; you are more likely to get the help you are looking for in return.

10. TWITTER

"Somewhere, something incredible is waiting to be known."
Carl Sagan

In this Chapter:
- ✓ Twitter can be very helpful for career or business research.
- ✓ It can also be helpful for getting meetings via replying to tweets of those you follow.
- ✓ Twitter's job search benefit is NOT primarily from building a following for your tweets.
- ✓ Twitter works well for certain professions, but not for others.
- ✓ You need to invest three or four hours experimenting with Twitter to see if it will work well for your target audience.
- ✓ Given this time investment and uncertain payoff, place Twitter further down on your list of things to do, and well-below getting set-up on LinkedIn.
- ✓ You need a free "Social Media Organizer" to use Twitter for research and career management.
- ✓ Find people and "lists" to follow by looking at those who tweet in your job target and seeing you they follow.

Twitter is a free service that enables its users to send and read messages known as *tweets*. These are messages of up to 140 characters that are displayed on the author's profile page and delivered to the author's subscribers who are known as *followers*. All users can send and receive tweets via the Twitter website or external applications.

Some people use Twitter to build a following via their tweets. Others use Twitter primarily to search for information or respond to the tweets of others to build relationships.

Caution: Tweeting to build a following can be time-consuming, with an uncertain payoff. For building business, building a following does make sense. For the job search, I believe there are better ways to spend your time. In both cases, however, using Twitter for research and to build relationships could hold substantial benefits, depending on your field, product or service.

In the immediate sections that follow, I will discuss Twitter from this research, relationship building perspective, since it is relevant to all the readers of this book. In the subsequent chapter on Prioritizing Social Media for Business, I will address building a following using Twitter in more detail.

Twitter for Research and Relationships

Not Every User will Benefit
Whether you should be on Twitter depends a lot on the nature of your target audience. Some targets lend themselves to doing research and building relationships via Twitter, others don't.

Twitter works best with targets that can be easily identified using certain keywords as search terms. For example, "marketing," "supply chain," "retail supply chain," "biotechnology," and "green tech" all work well with Twitter, because these simple words describe distinct practices and groups of people who have something to offer in these specialties.

On the other hand, if you only use the keywords "sales," "retail sales," or "finance" to describe your target, Twitter may be less useful to you. These terms are too broad, requiring too much precious time to sift through and find useful posts. "Sales" may turn up tweets from people trying to sell you something, rather than, for instance, people sharing knowledge about industry buyers in your field. "Finance" may generate tweets from people who want to be your personal financial advisor, when you're really looking for people who cover the latest issues in international corporate finance.

In addition, it may be that people in certain professions have a greater presence on Twitter than others. For example, the "social," "communication," and "tech-related" professions seem to gravitate toward Twitter, including information technology, marketing, sales, public relations, and entrepreneurs (including performing artists).

For those target audiences that are easily described and well represented, Twitter can be very helpful in advancing your job search or career. My advice: After you have picked the low-hanging fruit in your job search or career research, **spend three or four hours investigating Twitter to see if you can apply its unique features and benefits to your target audience**. If, after this time, you are feeling frustrated, then stop trying to make it work and move on to something else.

How Twitter Can Help
Twitter can be most helpful for:

- **Research**. Think of Twitter as a search portal for quickly and easily accessing the most up-to-date, relevant information for your job target or business.

    o Learn from leaders in your field about the latest developments, or what they are thinking and reading, nearly as fast as they are thinking or reading it!

    o Set up Twitter to make it far easier than conducting Google searches to identify and access the information you need.

- **Relationship-building**. Follow people you don't know (or those you do know) to possibly build or strengthen a professional relationship with them that could lead to referrals, meetings and interviews. You can comment on the tweets of others, and start a dialogue with people you would otherwise not have access to.

- **Getting the word out about your search**. If you can get someone with thousands of followers to tweet the thing you need— a job, for example, or a person with a specific skill set— that can be powerful! You may be able to accomplish this through relationships you build on Twitter, or just through asking someone you know in the "real world" with a following to tweet your request.

Getting Set-up on Twitter

Go to www.twitter.com and get your free User ID and password. For marketing purposes, try to have your full name comprise all or part of your User ID.[4]

Get a Social Media Manager

Next you will need a free **Social Media Manager** application, the filing system for tweets, to organize your tweets by job target, company, and the ways you are searching within each job target. These applications make it easy to spot useful information, and are essential when using Twitter for your research, as well as for tweeting across multiple social media platforms (more on that in Chapter 13).

Social media managers (SMMs) allow you to group tweets into columns defined by you—for example, you can have a company column or an industry column. You will need a separate user id and password for your SMM. Once it is set up, you will rarely need to go to your twitter.com home page.

These SMMs can be located on your desktop or online. Popular SMMs include *Buffer* and *Hootsuite* (and there are others). For demonstration purposes, I'll reference Hootsuite, which is the one I use.

Terms You Need to Know

Here are some of the basic terms you will come across when using Twitter through Hootsuite.

- **Lists:** These are compiled by Twitter users (anyone can create a public or private list), and group together people tweeting on a particular topic. The advantage of lists is that you can get all the tweets at once from individuals on the list; you don't have to follow each individual. One example of the many thousands of public lists people have put together is "CTO", that is, a list of corporate Chief Technology Officers who tweet.

---

[4] The concept is similar with your email address. If you have doggie23@hotmail.com as your primary email address, get a new one just for your job search with your full name in it, like paulmccartney@gmail.com.

- **Stream:** a column of tweets in Hootsuite that is generated by either search terms or the name of a Twitter list. All tweets in Hootsuite are separated into individual streams/columns. There are four types of streams:
    o **Stream:** a feed of all the tweets you have received or sent.
    o **Keyword:** a stream of tweets based on an individual keyword search.
    o **Search:** columns containing tweets filtered by phrases. You can use AND/OR connectors as well, such as "Merck AND Pfizer."
    o **Lists:** a stream that contains a public Twitter list you are following, or a list of tweeters that you are compiling yourself (public or private).

- **Tab:** A "filing cabinet" on Hootsuite that contains up to 10 streams.

- **Link Shorteners:** Website links can often be long. Since tweets are no longer than 140 characters, website link-shrinking is essential. Most SMMs can shrink your links for you if you enter the full link on the top of the screen (where you would tweet) and click "Shrink It." Online services such as http://ow.ly/url/shorten-url can also shrink your links for you.

- **Re-tweet, or RT:** This is a convention for "re-tweet." If you are passing on the information from someone else's tweet, it is common courtesy to add RT, and the username, within the tweet you are forwarding (that is, re-tweeting).

- **@username:** the @ sign signifies the Twitter name of the person. For me it would be @robhellmann. So, you might see "RT @robhellmann" followed by the tweet content.

- **Hashtags:** these reference the "#" character, as in #jobs, #marketing, etc. They signify user-created topics that catch on with a lot of users, and become conventions for searching by topic. For example, someone a few years ago decided that #jobs would mean tweets that link to job postings, and this convention caught on. See the Twitter resource links in the Appendix for popular hashtags.

Go to www.hootsuite.com, and get a free logon ID and password. Below you will find specifics on how to use Hootsuite, but first review Hootsuite's "help" resources, by clicking on the "Help" link at the bottom of its home page (or go directly to http://help.hootsuite.com/home). Also helpful is Twitter's support page at http://support.twitter.com/ .

Use a two-step approach to find relevant tweeters and organize their tweets.

1. **Search terms:** Set up separate streams of tweets within Hootsuite based on Twitter search terms. For example, you can set up search terms for company names, industries, or professions, and have separate streams of tweets for each of these.

2. **Examine Lists that others follow:** Using the search terms in step 1, you will identify people you want to follow. When you click on their Twitter profiles, you will see that many of them subscribe to, or have compiled on their own, Twitter "Lists" that contain tweeters covering a particular topic. You may decide to follow individuals on the list, just subscribe to the list, or do both.

Using Twitter - A Case Study

Let's use a client's job search to illustrate how Twitter can help you with your research and outreach. If you are not in a job search, it will be easy to translate these principles to your research and relationship-building needs.

Sarah's primary job target is Marketing Director for pharmaceutical companies in the Northeastern U.S. The top two companies she is targeting are Merck and Pfizer. Sarah wants Twitter to help her with:

- **Company Research:** Keeping current with the latest developments at Merck and Pfizer so that Sarah can use this information to get and ace interviews.
- **Research on Job Targets:** Keeping current on the latest trends in marketing in general, and pharma marketing in particular.
- **Networking:** Finding interesting or useful links that she can send to selected people in her network, as a way of keeping in

touch with them (e.g., someone she interviewed with a month ago for a position that may still be open). Also, develop and maintain relationships with people in a position to refer her, give advice, or hire her.

- **Making New Connections:** Contacting people at Merck or Pfizer whom she doesn't know in order to build relationships, which may lead to interviews.

Sarah sees Twitter as a way to 1) find valuable information that she might not have known about otherwise, 2) access information that she could have found elsewhere, but in a faster, easier way, on an ongoing basis, and 3) develop relationships helpful to her search that she might otherwise not have had an opportunity to develop.

Setting Up Twitter Search Streams

Sarah signed up for Twitter and Hootsuite, and viewed the Hootsuite help links. She then spent an hour experimenting with the correct search terms and keywords for setting up her initial streams (i.e. columns). On Hootsuite, Sarah clicked on the "add stream" button near the upper left and saw a new dialog box with four column-type choices, including "Stream", "Search", "Keyword" and "Lists" (picture that follows).

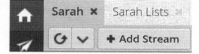

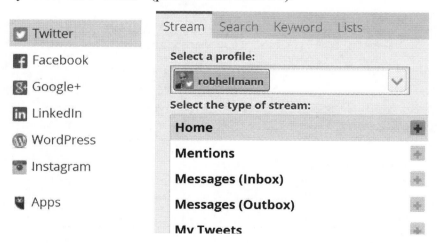

The dialog box also contains options to receive streams from many different social media sources, not just Twitter. Sarah made sure that "Twitter" was selected.

Sarah set up the following five columns (or streams):

1) A Keyword column that searched the word "Pfizer" for Pfizer's latest developments.
2) A Search column that searched the words "Pfizer Marketing" (meaning any tweet that contains both of the words "Pfizer" and "Marketing" within the tweet) for current news about Pfizer's marketing initiatives.
3) A Keyword column that searched the word "Merck."
4) A Search column that searched the words "Merck Marketing."
5) A Search column for "Pharma Marketing" for up-to-date marketing information on the pharmaceutical industry.

Let's look at a subset of the five columns more closely, as an illustration.

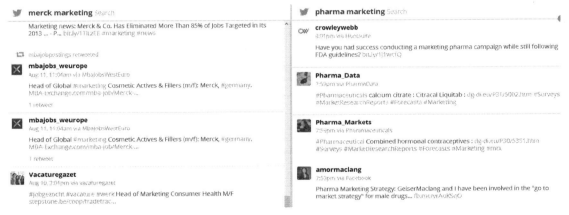

Search column "Merck Marketing"
The results, though similar to the "Merck" Keyword column, included additional useful tweets. For example: Merck's strategy of job eliminations.

Search column "Pharma Marketing"
Sarah found several tweets giving her useful information about her target industry. The tweets included links to articles on:
- Marketing campaigns that follow FDA guidelines
- Pharma go-to-market strategy
- An article on marketing analytics and pharma

Keyword column "Merck" (not pictured)

In this column, Sarah immediately spotted a few interesting tweets. These included:

- Several tweets about Merck's quarterly results.
- Critical overview of Merck's product pipeline.
- Numerous employment opportunity postings from "MerckJobs."

In one tweet, she also found a reference to a pharma marketing blog that she subscribed to, which was a valuable source for the latest industry gossip and information. In addition to the articles themselves, the tweets gave her links to new resources. For example, Sarah clicked on the link for Sigma Insights, the tweeter of the "Marketing Analytics and Pharma" article, and saw this:

Since Sarah found these tweets to be helpful to her job search, she decided to follow SIGMA_Insights, by clicking on "Follow" at the bottom left. She then created a new stream in Hootsuite, selected "lists" as the column type, called the column "Tweeters in Pharma Marketing," and added SIGMA_Insights as the first member to this list.

Searching for Individuals and Lists to Follow

Sarah found more individuals to follow by checking the Twitter profiles of those showing up in her Search Columns. For example, in addition to following SIGMA_Insights, she also started following Pharmagossip, whose tweets she found useful. When going to Pharmagossip's profile, she saw that Pharmagossip followed 11 lists:

TWEETS	FOLLOWING	FOLLOWERS	FAVORITES	LISTS
30.2K	5,970	16.3K	1,551	11

Sarah found additional individuals to follow by browsing the 11 lists, most of which were pharma-related. She also decided to subscribe to four of those eleven lists herself, including one list called "Pharma/biotech."

Now back on Hootsuite, she decided to create a new "Sarah lists" tab just for the lists she was following, while keeping her search columns in the "Sarah" tab. She did this by clicking on the "+" button to the right of the tabs, and then adding "Sarah lists". She then clicked on the "+Add Stream" icon on the upper left, selected "lists", and picked the "Pharma/biotech" list she just subscribed to from the dropdown menu.

Sarah added some of the pharma tweeters she was now finding to her own list. For example. In Hootsuite, she decided to add Pharmagossip to her "Tweeters in Pharma Marketing" list. She did this by simply clicking on the "Pharmagossip" link in one of the tweets, and at the bottom-right of the resulting stream of tweets clicking "Add to List."

Making New Connections: Sarah noticed one particular tweet, from a pharmaceutical marketing director that she was now following. He tweeted about the hard day he was having due to a recent pharma announcement. So Sarah went to the post, and clicked on the "Direct Message" icon to right of the tweet to send a personal message that only the tweeter would see.

Sarah was pleasantly surprised when she quickly got an appreciative response. She knew she would want to keep in touch via Twitter, in the hopes of leveraging this contact for an informational meeting or additional introductions to others in the company.

For one last check, Sarah went back to the main Twitter home page, to see if Twitter might make additional suggestions on who to follow, now that she was following a few people and lists. She clicked on "Who to Follow" on the left column, and decided to follow some of the suggestions offered.

Conclusion: In three hours Sarah succeeded in setting up a system on Twitter that would accomplish her objectives of 1) learning new, valuable information she wouldn't have known about, 2) accessing information more easily, and 3) developing new professional relationships.

Sarah's example should demonstrate how you can use Twitter to advance your job search, business or career. As you can see, experimentation and effort are required to find the correct search terms for your job target, and people or lists to follow.

Careful: Look before you Tweet!

If you tweet to your followers or reply to a tweet, remember that once you press "Send-Now" everyone can see your post! If you mean to send a private message, make sure you hit the "Direct Message" button, and not "Reply."

You can, however, delete an errant tweet so that it will disappear from your followers' feeds and search engines. Here's what you do:

1. Log in to Twitter at www.twitter.com.
2. Visit your profile.
3. Locate the tweet that you want to delete.
4. Click the trash can on the lower right corner of the tweet.

Deleted tweets can linger in Twitter search. They will clear with time.

An Errant Tweet

11. BLOGS

"If you can't explain it simply, you don't understand it well enough."
Albert Einstein

In this Chapter:
✓ Follow the blogs of leaders in your field to learn about the latest developments that will help you land opportunities.
✓ Consider using the "comments" section of a blog to establish a dialogue with a blogger who may be able to help you.
✓ Don't blog regularly for a job-search unless it really comes easily to you.
✓ Do consider writing an occasional blog entry to demonstrate your expertise and currency in your field.

What is a Blog?
A blog is "a type of website, usually maintained by an individual with regular entries of commentary, descriptions of events, or other material such as graphics or video." *(Wikipedia)*

Blogs enable anyone to become writers, journalists, or publishers. There are several free sites that allow you to quickly get started with blogging, including www.tumblr.com and www.wordpress.com.

Blogs are commonly incorporated into existing websites, as mine is. You can use blogs to help advance your career by:
- Writing your own blog
- Reading other people's blogs
- Commenting on other people's blogs

Writing Your Own Blog
Bloggers usually want to draw attention to their blog and build a following, which means they have to update their blog at least once a week (and sometimes several times a day). Unless you have your own

business (more on that in Chapter 13), do not seek to write and update a blog this often, unless blogging comes very easily to you, or your job target involves writing your opinions frequently and under deadline. There are better ways to spend your valuable job-search and career-advancement time.

You may want to write just one or two blog entries, however, or just update your blog occasionally (say once a month). You will not be building a following this way, but you can use these infrequent entries to show that you are current and knowledgeable in your field. Consider this approach if:

- You have been out of work for a while.
- You are seeking to make a career or industry change.
- The knowledge needed for success in your field is changing rapidly.

One of my clients began a blog in her field: Supply Chain Management. She wrote just one entry to demonstrate that she is current in her field. She wrote about new Federal regulations and how they would impact supply chain managers. The link to her blog, which she included in her email signature and LinkedIn profile, caught the attention of hiring managers at a company she was applying to work in, and ultimately led to a job offer. The hiring managers said that this one blog entry played a critical role in their decision-making.

Naming Your Blog
If you do decide to write your own blog, have your name in the blog website address to most effectively market yourself. (WordPress will give you instructions on how to do that as you register). The job search is about marketing yourself, and your name is the name of "your product."

Reading Other People's Blogs
Subscribe to blogs that can help you to research your target, including companies where you would like to work, competitors, or thought leaders in your field.

One place to find relevant blogs is at "Best of the Web Blog Search" (http://blogs.botw.org/) where you can find a highly selective, curated list. Another way to search is by going to blogsearch.google.com, but it will take you a lot of time to wade through all of your search results, and you may still not find what you are looking for.

So, how do you quickly find the best blogs to follow for your job target? I always advocate starting with the obvious, easy things first. For example, I googled "Best Marketing blog" and within five minutes identified top blogs and useful information that would be very helpful in generating interviews for a marketing position.

Another great way to find the best blogs is by asking professionals in your profession or industry what they read. Use your LinkedIn groups or associations you are affiliated with to ask these questions. Or, see what blogs people in your field are tweeting about.

Replying to the Blogs of Others

When you follow the blogs of leaders in your field, engage them in an intelligent, appropriate way, via leaving blog "comments". Start online conversations that could perhaps lead to building new professional relationships.

Keeping Track of Blogs with "Feed Readers"

You may have noticed that most blogs and many news sites display an orange icon that looks like this: This "RSS feed" icon indicates that the content is available for inclusion in a "feed reader." This web application makes it very easy to scan a large number of blogs and news reports quickly for information that interests you. Readers are one of the best ways of keeping on top of the voluminous information that is available to you as you research your target audience.

One of the most popular feed readers is "Feedly." Go to www.feedly.com and open a free Reader account there.

Once you have your account set up, you can enter websites on Feedly or go to a blog or news source that displays the RSS feed icon, and click on it. For example, in Feedly you can enter www.hellmannconsulting.com/blog to add a feed to read my blog posts, or www.inc.com or www.nytimes.com to get feeds from these websites. Then just click the green "+feedly" button to add the feed, and it will prompt for the folder in which you want to save the feed.

  🔍 www.nytimes.com   ✕

| 🔖 | NYT > Home Pa... | 25 | **German Parliament Overwhelmingly Approves Greek Bailout** | 56min |
| 🔖 | NYT > Home Pa... | 24 | **City Room: New York Today: The Mayor and the Media**   Wednesday: | 1h |

Feedly will also suggest popular feeds that are similar to those you subscribe to, as another way of identifying blogs involving your job target. Posts can often be read within the reader itself—that is, you don't have to open a ton of web pages as you read through the posts.

You can create folders and tags in the reader and sort and organize your feeds for easy browsing. For example, I have a folder I call "Career Services News" that contains career-related feeds. Or I can simply do a search across all my feeds using the word "Career," which often works better than folders and tags for identifying articles of interest.

The First Blog

12. FACEBOOK

"I would rather walk with a friend in the dark, than alone in the light."
Helen Keller

In this Chapter:

✓ Facebook is primarily social by nature, which makes it less useful for career management; fJit is not a substitute for LinkedIn!

✓ If you already have a substantial network on Facebook, use it to let your network know about your job search.

✓ If you are not already a heavy user of Facebook, do not invest time with this platform just for your career.

✓ Facebook Business Pages can be very useful in building a business or an audience.

Facebook now has well over a billion users. Go to www.facebook.com to sign up for this free service. Facebook allows users to add people as "friends," in order to send them messages and updates on their personal profiles. Additionally, users can join networks organized by workplace, school, or profession.

If you do not use Facebook regularly, then I don't recommend immersing yourself more deeply in it just for your career or business. Because Facebook's primary use is social in nature (as opposed to professional), it is often not good etiquette to contact someone you don't really know about target research or an informational meeting. It could be off-putting. In addition, if you have been using Facebook for maintaining contact with close friends and family, it will feel inappropriate to all parties involved (including your new business "friends") to start bringing business contacts into this circle. **LinkedIn is the place to do this kind of professional outreach.**

If you are already on Facebook, however, and are using it actively to keep in touch with people, then use Facebook to tell your network of Facebook "friends" about your job search, new business venture, etc. In that context, Facebook could be very useful for letting your network know how they can help you. Also, take a look at Facebook groups, described next.

Facebook Groups

These groups are similar to LinkedIn groups in that they are a place for registered users who share a particular interest, profession, or association. They are not as tailored, however, as LinkedIn groups are for the job search. Nevertheless, they could place you in a community that could help you build new career-advancing relationships.

Here's how you find and join a Facebook group. Log into Facebook and go to the search box on top. Type in "Groups named Art Director" for example (or whatever other phrase represents your job target).

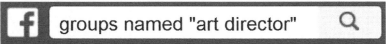

Press enter, and you find a list of Facebook Groups that have both the words "Art" and "Director" as part of their names. Click on the group's name to access its homepage. To join the group, click the "Like" button at the top of the page.

To see for yourself the difference between Facebook groups and LinkedIn groups, you can try typing in "Art Director" yourself on the group searches of both applications. You will immediately be struck by the differences in group quality for "Art Director" between the two applications: the LinkedIn groups for Art Director have far more members and more current, active useful discussions on the profession. My own research, and the feedback I receive from clients, suggests that LinkedIn generally has more and better business-networking oriented groups.

In addition, I find the experience of searching for groups on Facebook to be frustrating because you can't fine-tune your search results the way you can on LinkedIn. You will probably scroll through many "frogs" before you find that "prince" of a group that you want to join.

Facebook Pages

One final thought: Facebook can potentially be very helpful if you are trying to build a business or an audience for events, provided that a significant segment of your potential customers tend to also be on Facebook. You can attract attention to your business by setting up a "Business Page" that could drive traffic to your business. I know of clients and colleagues that have done very well advertising their events or attracting new customers via these business pages. See Chapter 13 for more information on Facebook pages and building a business.

Anti-Social Media

13. SOCIAL MEDIA FOR YOUR BUSINESS

"I keep track of my blog stats, Facebook subs, my Amazon rank, Twitter followers, Facebook likes per posts, my chess ranking. I get stressed when they all don't go up."
James Altucher

For the job search and general career advancement activities, LinkedIn is king for all the reasons we've already covered. If you are trying to build a business, however, LinkedIn's relative importance may drop. Social media can help your business get the word out about your product or service through **building a following**. If you think about it this way, then the platform you prioritize will depend on where your clients or customers are. LinkedIn might be the priority, or it might be Facebook, Twitter, Pinterest, Foursquare, or even (and often) old fashioned email!

One word of caution, however, regarding using social media for building a following for your business. First, consider how social media should fit into your overall marketing priorities. Doing social media right for your business is time consuming! If you are a solopreneur, you probably won't be able to do it all. Figure out how you want to prioritize your time among three marketing channels. Consider focusing on just one channel, and doing it really well:

- Giving Talks
- Writing
- Social Media

Examples of Building a Following

Successful social media initiatives for business have involved followings of hundreds, thousands or even millions of people. I've seen clients and colleagues use their large followings to fill their events, increase usage of their services, and publicize new product launches. Here are a few quick examples:

❖ A colleague of mine fills all of her career services classes via status updates to her thousands of Facebook Page followers.

❖ A photographer gets most of her business through her wide circle of Facebook friends, as she regularly posts photos to Facebook that generate hundreds of 'likes.'

❖ My sporadic blog posts have still been enough to bring in substantial new business, including several paid speaking engagements, media opportunities, and new clients.

❖ A book published in 2012 achieved #1 ranking on both Amazon and Barnes & Noble in June of 2011, **while the author was still writing it!** How? He tweeted about the book to his 1.1 million Twitter followers, and also shared it on some smaller online communities.[5]

The key to success in developing an engaged following is to add real value, with sincerity, in your social media interactions. Share useful links, solid advice, or promotions and discounts. Or be very witty.

We have already discussed how you might go about building a following within LinkedIn in Chapter 5, "For Your Business…" Here are some high level thoughts on how additional social media applications can help you to build a following.

Facebook
This platform works very well for building a following because of its enormous user base and features for posting to followers. You will need to set up a Facebook business "Page" in addition to your personal page. A Facebook Page is a Facebook-specific website for your business. These pages are becoming fairly sophisticated. In fact, some businesses are forgoing regular websites altogether to focus on their Facebook page! My very basic Facebook page is at www.facebook.com/hcconsulting.

---

[5] Read about this in the Wall Street Journal (http://on.wsj.com/s8bKSj) and at Mashable (http://mashable.com/2011/08/01/authors-social-media/).

Since this section is meant as a high level overview, I'll outsource the mechanics of setting up a Facebook page to Facebook's own page creation site: http://www.facebook.com/pages/create.php. You may need to log into your Facebook personal profile first. Creating a basic page is fairly easy and straightforward.

Once your page is set up, post content that is valuable to your target audience on the page status feed, and get people to follow you by "liking" your page (i.e. pressing the "Like" button). Successful Facebook pages can have thousands or millions of followers. By interspersing notices of your events or services within the helpful postings, you can generate additional revenue.

Twitter
Similarly, use Twitter to build a following 140 characters at a time. Consider three ways of using Twitter to build a following:
- Tweet useful links to those who could be your customers or clients, as if you were curating a reading list. Feedly (see Chapter 11, page 121) makes it easy to quickly find interesting articles or blog posts that you would want to tweet to your followers.
- Tweet your own content, for example, excerpts from your blog posts.
- Re-tweet the content of others. Those whose content you re-tweet may decide to follow you.

Blogs
To successfully build a following with a blog, you have to write a post at least once a week (many bloggers post several times a day). Blogs can be time consuming to write. I have a blog on my website (www.hellmannconsulting.com/blog) but I update it a couple of times a month, not enough to build a following.

My blog has, however, served two business-building purposes despite these infrequent updates: 1) the information I provide in blog posts has been a valuable resource for clients and prospects, raising the profile of my website as a destination for people looking for the kind of help I can offer, and 2) I'm demonstrating expertise with my blog posts, which has helped to communicate value to potential purchasers of my services.

Email Lists and other Online Groups

Email Lists, Yahoo Groups, LinkedIn Groups, and other specialty groups organized around a shared interest can be great for getting the word out to group members who could either buy your service directly or let others know about it. The key is to remember that the best groups are communities that are valued by the participants, where people help each other. So, be a resource to the other members! Don't overtly sell in these groups—you will be ostracized and quite possibly banned from the group if you are constantly hawking your "Seven Ways to…" book.

Instead, invest time in becoming a helpful presence within the group. Tactfully mention your service only on occasion and perhaps via a one-to-one message. Include a link to your product or service in the signature of your email or group posting. If you're pushy in a group, you will rightfully be pushed out.

Here are a couple of examples. I'm in a small specialty group for the contact management system I use. One of the regular posters, a source of useful help and information to the others, discreetly sells an email management service that is targeted to this audience. Over time, he has built up quite a positive reputation, as well as a substantial revenue stream, just from this little group.

Another colleague is co-president of a small startup company making affordable professional speakers for music enthusiasts and hobbyists. Virtually all their substantial revenue came initially from this kind of helpful, discreet, long-term participation in a forum for do-it-yourself recording artists.

Post to Several Applications at Once

Save time and have one posting go to all of your social media applications at once by posting via Hootsuite or other social media managers (See Chapter 10 ("Twitter"), page 110 for more information). For example, when I have something to share with followers, I will post it via Hootsuite to my Twitter feed, my LinkedIn profile-status-update, my Facebook page, and my Facebook personal profile all at the same time! For this to work, the post needs to be 140 characters maximum, since that's the maximum number of characters that Twitter allows.

Guidelines for Posting
The general rule for social media postings: first quality (i.e. useful posts), then quantity. Here's what to say "yes" and "no" to:

YES: Postings of value, usually links to useful articles, discounts or advice that's really a value-add.

YES: Occasional announcements of your products or events: no more than one product reminder for every four helpful posts.

YES: Occasional requests for help.

YES: Posting at least once a day.

YES: Throw in something personal every so often—so people can relate to you—especially if your business is you!

NO: Too many posts that very few people care about (e.g. too much back and forth on Twitter).

NO: Relentless selling.

Final Thoughts on Prioritizing Applications
The key rule to remember in prioritizing your social media efforts is to focus on the communication channels that are most likely to reach your customers.

For example, if the market for your business-to-business technology solution includes Senior VPs of Information Technology, that audience may be more attuned to Twitter (it has a more hi-tech cachet) or LinkedIn (more "professional") than to Facebook. One-on-one outreach to sell your services to other executives and organizational decision-makers also may result in your prioritizing your LinkedIn network over building a following.

14. GOOGLE YOURSELF

*"It takes many good deeds to build a good reputation,
and one bad one to lose it."*
Benjamin Franklin

LinkedIn can help you to show up more prominently in Google's search results, which is great if you are looking for a job or trying to build your business. On the other hand, your presence in other social media may also show up in Google searches, with perhaps less than optimal results.

Type your name into Google and see what comes up (that's what many recruiters and hiring managers do). What do you find? Hopefully nothing bad; no embarrassing pictures from earlier days. When I google myself I find my career coaching website, my LinkedIn and Twitter profiles, my blog, an article I wrote, and an old website I created containing some music compositions. Phew, nothing embarrassing here! What if you don't like what comes up? Try these suggestions:

- Un-tag yourself from embarrassing Facebook photos.
- Ask the host to take down the information.
- Restrict the privacy on your Facebook settings to your true "friends."
- Create your job-search profiles (e.g. LinkedIn, Twitter, Blogs, etc.) with a slightly different name (e.g. a middle initial, your maiden name) so they will not be connected to you.
- Put enough new information up on the web that the old, "bad" information gets buried.
- Do a search on the Internet for reputation "cleaners"—vet them carefully!
- Going forward, be careful about what you post on Facebook, etc. (including what you write) and monitor or restrict what others post about you.

Although a detailed review of how to protect and clean up your reputation is beyond the scope of this book, this subject is not to be taken lightly. A lot of information exists on the web about this topic if you need to know more: just enter "online reputation" in Google.

APPENDIX 1: ADDITIONAL RESOURCES

General Career Management

www.hellmannconsulting.com : *Hellmann Career Consulting*, the website for my career coaching practice. On this site, you'll find:

- ✓ The archive for my Career blog, which offers advice on a range issues spanning the job search, career change, and success on the job.
- ✓ A Career Links page, with all links tested by me. Use these links for essential job target research.
- ✓ A Seminars page which lists seminars and webinars (some of them recorded) on the job search and career management that I lead, most of which are open to the public.

www.fiveoclockclub.com : *The Five O'Clock Club*'s job search methodology has been referenced repeatedly in this book, and is second to none. On this site you'll find a variety of career resources as well as the ability to join their fee-based weekly job search groups.

Resources that Help You Use Twitter

Twitter is not just a self-contained platform like LinkedIn. In order to use it most effectively, you need to go outside of Twitter to the numerous external applications and Twitter directories on the web. Here's a sample listing.

- Popular **Social Media Managers** include (there are many others):
  - o www.hootsuite.com
  - o www.bufferapp.com
  - o www.socialoomph.com
  - o www.agorapulse.com
  - o www.sproutsocial.com

- A guide to Twitter Acronyms: http://www.labnol.org/internet/popular-twitter-acronyms/6819/
- A resource guide to Twitter: http://www.twitip.com/
- Search Twitter Job Postings: http://jobmob.co.il/blog/twitter-job-openings-postings-leads/ List of Twitter job feeds globally, by type of industry/profession.

Sites that Facilitate Social Media Posting

These sites do things like allow you to post in one place to multiple social media sites, view all your social media activity from one portal, shorten URLs, and so forth.

- www.hootsuite.com
- www.tweetdeck.com
- www.bufferapp.com
- www.onlywire.com Allows posting to 52 different social networks (e.g. LinkedIn, Twitter, Facebook, etc.). Low monthly charge.
- http://www.linksalpha.com/ : enables you to publish to multiple social media applications (inexpensive)
- http://bit.ly/ : URL shortener.
- http://ow.ly/url/shorten-url : URL shortener.

Articles and how-to's on Social Media
www.mashable.com

Other Online Social Media Sites

www.foursquare.com : Popular with companies building their "brick & mortar" business and brand.

www.google.com/+ : Google+, Google's answer to Facebook.

www.yahoogroups.com : If you can find the right group, this portal could be very helpful in learning about your target. Yahoo groups are more like email lists than LinkedIn groups.

www.pinterest.com : Pinterest is a personalized media platform with a huge social component. Users can manage images and other media (i.e. videos) through collections. Very popular now with those who have something "visual" to say.

www.instagram.com : another very popular social media platform for those wanting to share visual media.

APPENDIX 2: EIGHT RULES FOR WRITING GREAT LETTERS

Every so often I hear the comment that "nobody reads cover letters." That's because most of the letters jobseekers send are just too hard to get through! Follow these rules and not only will your letter be read, but you'll greatly improve the odds of getting the result you want.

Rule #1: Make your letter easily "scannable"
These days, work is too fast-paced to allow for reading through a long, dense letter. DON'T take a page out of your English Literature 101 class. Instead, make your letter a quick, easy read by:

- Using short paragraphs– no more than seven lines in any one paragraph (assuming an 8.5×11 Word document). Less than seven lines is better.
- Using bullet points (e.g. like this).
- Using bold-face and/or <u>underlining</u> of key phrases to bring them out. Make sure you use this technique sparingly– if too much is in bold or underlined, it will defeat the purpose and look terrible.
- Considering the use of sub-headings. This blog post, with its use of the "rules" subheadings, is an example.
- Minimizing repetition. You don't need to mention your extensive marketing background three times– once is enough. So make sure you minimize repetition.

Rule #2: Default to using email
Start with the presumption that you are going to write your letter of introduction, cover letter, or interview/meeting follow-up as an email, then "convince yourself" why using postal mail would be better. The reasons you want to default to email: first, it works (as I see every day with clients), and second, sending an email is so much faster. You can skip finding/buying stamps, getting the envelope to print properly, and remembering to mail the letter (it usually takes me about three days!). The table below summarizes the pros and cons of sending an email vs. mailing a letter.

Email vs. Postal Mail in a Job Search: Pros vs. Cons

Email		Letter by Postal Mail	
✓	Fast for you	X	Time consuming
✓	Easy to respond	X	Hard to respond
✓	Everyone reads email	X	Delay in getting/reading mail
✓	Quick Delivery	X	Longer Delivery
✓	It works!	✓	It works!
X	Spam Issues	✓	No Spam Issues
X	Just another email	✓	Stands Out
❖	More Current	❖	More Old School
❖ symbol means "pros/cons depend on the recipient"			

Your job search time is valuable. Perhaps you've heard of the expression "the perfect is the enemy of the good." There's so much that you need to do in a job search, so go for "good" or even "great" in your search and let go of "perfect."

That said, there are several situations where sending a letter by mail will get you a better result.

1. If you've had an informational or networking meeting and someone really helped you, a handwritten note of appreciation is a very nice touch!
2. If you feel the person to whom you are reaching out is more "old school," e.g. from an older generation, more conservative, etc. then a letter may be more appropriate.
3. A letter will stand out more than an email will, improving the odds of it being read. To help a letter stand out even more, consider sending it by "Priority Mail." If you have the time, you could send an email and, if no response, then a letter.

Rule #3: Always include the "letter" in the body of the email, as people don't like to open attachments. Enough said.

Rule #4: Engage them with the Email Subject Line
If you do use email, the subject line is key to your message being read. Don't make it too salesy or pushy. Mention something that they are interested in so that your email gets opened! Examples include:

- "Your article about Supply Chain in…"
- "Referred by Susan Smith, re:…"
- "Open to discussing Fundraising at Ivy University?"
- "Our three mutual connections and shared group on LinkedIn"
- "Hello, and question…" <if you know them>

Rule #5: Make sure your email address is professional
doggie23@hotmail.com won't cut it. firstnamelastname@gmail.com will make a better impression and make you more likely to get past the spam filters.

Rule #6: Focus on them
I get so many drafts that are all about "me me me" when the tone/language should be "here's how I can help you…" , "I believe this meeting would be mutually beneficial because…" or "Your company's Vision resonates…" If you want them to help you, show appreciation, as in "I would greatly appreciate…" A simple "thank you" can of course go a long way. Sounds easy and obvious but too many clients forget these basic rules of relationships.

Rule #7: Include your pitch (if you haven't in a prior letter)
Inform the people to whom you are writing of your background and link it to how you can help them. Summarize your background in one or two sentences, and then share some relevant background highlights by including three to six "bulleted" accomplishments. Don't assume that even your best, closest work colleague knows how you want to position yourself, or remembers the great things you've done. Also, strangers will naturally want to know from whom they are hearing. A powerful pitch in your email can really help to illustrate how you can help an organization, engage the reader, and spur the action you want.

Rule #8: End with a clear call to action
Say "Would you have 20 minutes available on your calendar to meet?" (it's so easy for them to hit reply on an email and say yes.) And/or, say "I'll contact your office to see if I can get on your calendar in a few days, assuming I don't hear from you first."

I'll be posting more in the near future about how to write great email content that gets you the meetings you want, as well has how to follow up with a phone call.

GLOSSARY OF TERMS

@username: (Twitter) the @ sign signifies the Twitter name of the person. For me it would be @robhellmann.

1st Degree Network: (LinkedIn) The people you connect with directly.

2nd Degree Network: (LinkedIn) The people who connect directly with your 1st degree network.

3rd Degree Network: (LinkedIn) The people who connect directly with your 2nd degree network.

Blog: "a type of website, usually maintained by an individual with regular entries of commentary, descriptions of events, or other material such as graphics or video." (Wikipedia)

Email Lists: (also referred to as electronic mailing lists) Messages among individuals who subscribe to the list that form conversations around specific topics. These conversations can be archived and are searchable.

Facebook: A social media application that allows users to add people as "friends," in order to send them messages and updates on their personal profiles. Additionally, users can join networks organized by workplace, school, or profession.

Feed: (Twitter) a stream of all the tweets you have received or sent.

Group: LinkedIn members who congregate in an organized LinkedIn forum around a specific topic, profession, or association.

Hashtags: (Twitter) These reference the "#" character, as in #jobs, #marketing, etc. They signify user-created topics that catch on with a lot of users, and become conventions for searching by topic.

Job Board: Websites that contain online ads for job openings. www.indeed.com is one such job board, and there are many others. Go to the links page on my website (scroll down) to see more.

Keyword: (Twitter) a stream of tweets based on an individual keyword search.

Link Shorteners: (Twitter) since tweets are no longer than 140 characters, link shrinking is essential. Most Twitter organizers can shrink your links for you if you enter the full link on the top of the screen (where you would tweet) and click "Shrink It." Online services such as http://ow.ly/url/shorten-url can also shrink your links for you.

LinkedIn: a service accessed at www.linkedin.com that enables users to keep in touch with and expand their professional network, get introductions to others outside their immediate network, and join groups of professionals organized around industries, professions, and associations.

Lists stream: a Twitter organizer column that contains a public Twitter list you are following, or a list of tweeters that you are compiling yourself (public or private).

Lists: Compiled by Twitter users (anyone can create a public or private list), and aggregate people tweeting on a particular topic. The advantage of lists is that you can get all the tweets at once from individuals on the list—you don't have to follow each individual.

Networking: Building and maintaining relationships over time that can lead to interviews or referrals. The key is to **keep in touch** with people that you meet.

Pitch (or elevator speech): a concise statement about how you would be valuable to an employer or potential client/customer. See my book *PEAK Presentations* (www.hellmannconsulting.com/book) to learn how to create a great pitch.

RT (re-tweet): (Twitter) a convention for "re-tweet." If you are passing on the information from someone else's tweet, it is common courtesy to add RT, and the username, within the tweet you are forwarding (that is, re-tweeting).

Search columns: (Twitter) Search columns allow searching by phrases, using connections such as "And," "Or," and so forth.

Social Media: Primarily online or mobile media that enables conversation and interaction between people.

Social Media Dashboard: Organizes social media posts that you are monitoring, from different platforms (e.g. Twitter, Facebook, LinkedIn, etc.) into columns, or "filing cabinets." Enables you to post to multiple platforms from one place. Hootsuite is a popular example.

Stream: (Twitter) a column of tweets (or posts from other applications) in Hootsuite that is generated by search terms or the name of a Twitter list. All tweets in Hootsuite are separated into individual streams/columns.

Tab: (Twitter) a category on Hootsuite that contains up to 10 streams (or columns).

Tweep: (Twitter) a follower on Twitter.

Twitter: a free service at www.twitter.com that enables its users to send and read messages known as tweets. These are messages of up to 140 characters that are displayed on the author's profile page and delivered to the author's subscribers who are known as followers. All users can send and receive tweets via the Twitter website or external applications.

Word cloud: enables you to visually see the frequency of words that show up in a block of text. If you google "Word Cloud" you will see the many free tools that can enable you to create word clouds. I use "TagCrowd" at www.tagcrowd.com. Word clouds are helpful in identifying keywords for your resume or LinkedIn profile.

Your purchase of this book entitles you to download the digital eBook for this edition, for free!

To download the book, follow these steps.

1. Go to the "book" page of my website: http://hellmannconsulting.com/book

2. Click the "Buy" button for the eBook.

3. Enter "**newinterface**" in the discount window (without the quotes).

4. Click "update cart," then "checkout."

NOTES PAGE

Made in the USA
Columbia, SC
28 April 2017